The Wayland Junior
ILLUSTRATED
ATLAS

WRITTEN BY
SHIRLEY WILLIS

ILLUSTRATED BY
NICK HEWETSON

CREATED AND DESIGNED BY
DAVID SALARIYA

WAYLAND

Contents

ARCTIC 60

CANADA AND
GREENLAND
10-11

USA: THE WEST
AND MIDWEST
12-13

USA: THE MIDWEST
AND NORTHEAST
14-15

USA: THE SOUTH
16-17

MEXICO, CENTRAL
AMERICA AND CARIBBEAN
18-19

SOUTH AMERICA 20-21

BELGIUM, THE
NETHERLANDS AND
LUXEMBOURG 30-31

SCANDINAVIA,
FINLAND AND
ICELAND 22-23

GERMANY, AUSTRIA
AND SWITZERLAND
32-33

BRITISH
ISLES
24-25

CENTRAL AND
EASTERN EUROPE
38-39

FRANCE
28-29

GREECE 36-37

ITALY AND
MALTA 34-35

SOUTH-WEST
ASIA 42-43

SPAIN AND
PORTUGAL 26-27

NORTHERN EURASIA 40-41

CHINA, MONGOLIA, KOREA
AND TAIWAN 54-55

JAPAN
50-51

INDIA AND ITS
NEIGHBOURS 48-49

NORTHERN AFRICA 44-45

SOUTHEAST ASIA
52-53

SOUTHERN
AFRICA 46-47

SOUTH
WESTERN
PACIFIC
ISLANDS 59

AUSTRALIA AND PAPUA
NEW GUINEA 56-57

NEW ZEALAND
58

ANTARCTIC 61

3

The Earth in space

The Earth is a ball of rock that orbits the Sun. It depends on the Sun's energy for warmth and light.

The Earth is one of nine planets that orbit (circle) the Sun. Together they form the Solar System. Each planet orbits the Sun in an elliptical (oval) path. The length of a planet's orbit depends on its distance from the Sun. Mercury is closest and takes 88 days to orbit the Sun but Pluto takes 250 years because it is the outermost planet in our Solar System. The Earth's orbit takes about 365 days.

Neptune

Uranus

Saturn

Pluto

The Earth is always moving. As it orbits the Sun, the planet spins on its axis, making one complete turn every 24 hours. As one side of its surface is lit by the Sun, the other side is in darkness. This is why we have daytime and night-time.

The Earth's axis is an imaginary line running through its centre.

axis

The Earth seen from space.

The Earth is 148,800,000 km from the Sun, making it neither too hot nor too cold. It is the only planet in the Solar System where life is known to exist.

Mercury

Venus

Earth

Mars

Sun

Jupiter

From space, the Earth is seen as a huge round ball. The planet looks blue because much of its surface is covered in oceans. Large land masses, called continents, can also be seen. Closer up, the Earth looks flat. From an aeroplane, the towns, roads, rivers and railtracks below divide the countryside into a huge patchwork pattern. People are too small to be seen from this distance. If you look down from a skyscraper, people below can be seen but look as small as ants. Cars on the streets look like children's toys.

The Earth seen from an aeroplane.

The Earth seen from a tall building.

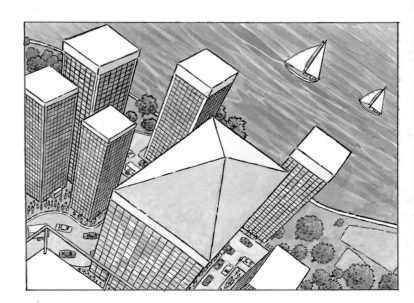

How the world becomes a flat map

A globe is a round map of the world. Map-makers make a flat map of the world for an atlas.

Our planet is made up of four layers (below). The surface of the Earth, on which we live, is called the crust. Every continent and ocean lies on the Earth's crust. Beneath the crust is a layer of rock called the mantle. Parts of the mantle are hot and molten (liquid) and can break through the crust to form a volcano. The core of the planet has two parts: the outer core is hot, molten metal and the inner core is solid metal.

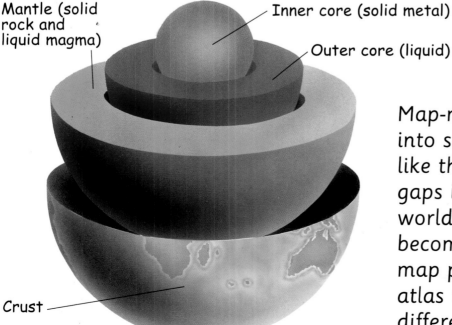

Mantle (solid rock and liquid magma)

Inner core (solid metal)

Outer core (liquid)

Crust

Map-makers divide the world's surface into segments. These are laid side by side like the skin of an orange, but this leaves gaps in the map (above). Parts of the world are 'stretched' so that the map becomes whole. This process is called map projection. On the flat maps in an atlas the countries are shaped slightly differently than they are on a globe.

Map-makers use a grid of imaginary lines across the globe to help plot the exact positions of places. Lines of longitude are drawn from north to south and lines of latitude from east to west.

The equator is an imaginary line dividing the world in half. It is positioned at latitude 0° (zero degrees). The northern hemisphere is above it and the southern hemisphere below.

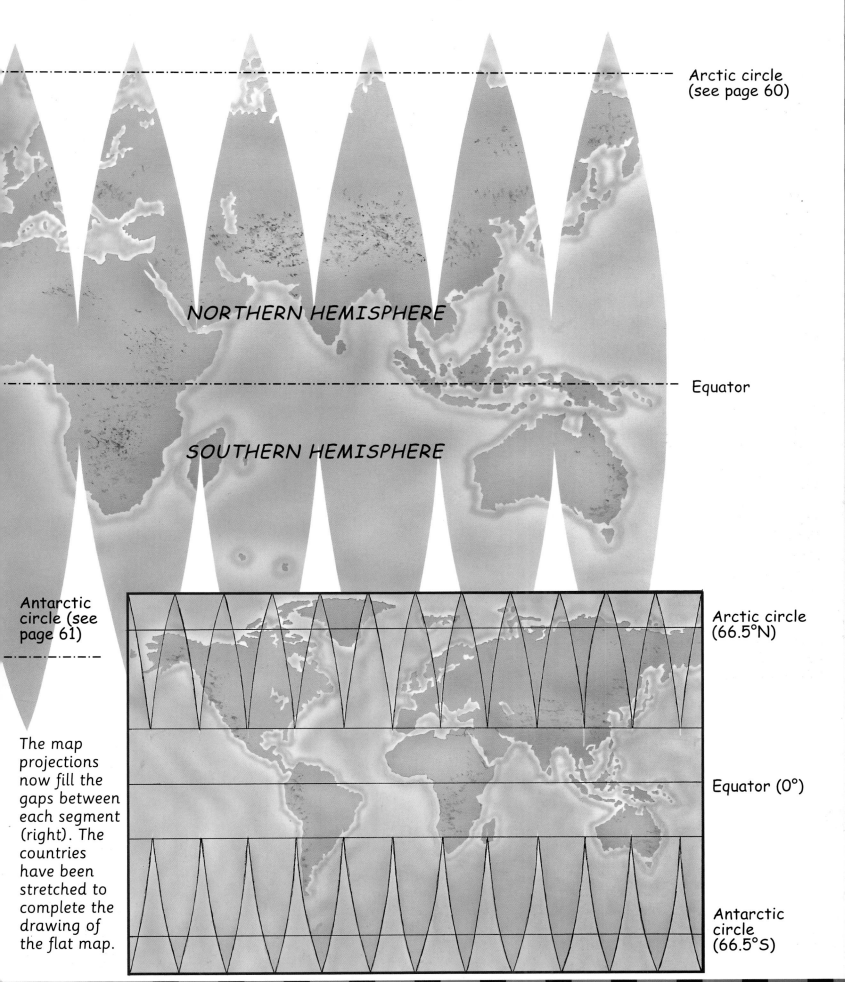

Arctic circle
(see page 60)

NORTHERN HEMISPHERE

Equator

SOUTHERN HEMISPHERE

Antarctic circle (see page 61)

Arctic circle
(66.5°N)

Equator (0°)

The map projections now fill the gaps between each segment (right). The countries have been stretched to complete the drawing of the flat map.

Antarctic circle
(66.5°S)

How the pages work in this atlas

This is the kind of map you will find in this atlas. Each page shows a map of different countries of the world. The notes on this page explain the type of information given on each map.

Look on the map for buildings or other places of interest that are shown in the 'Can you find...' box.

A large, bold label in capital letters shows a country's name.

A thick dotted line shows the border between countries. A thin dotted line shows the border of states within a country.

The globe shows where the countries on each map are in the world.

A small label like this shows the name of a lake or river.

A curved label like this shows the name of the sea or ocean.

Go to the fact box for extra information about each country or continent.

Scandinavia, F and Iceland

Norway, Sweden and Denmark are known as Scandinavia. These countries are rich in natural resources: timber, fish, oil and natural gas. They have warm summers but bitterly cold winters.

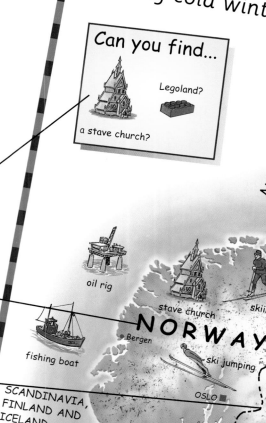

Can you find...

Legoland?

a stave church?

oil rig

stave church

skiing

NORWAY

Bergen

fishing boat

ski jumping

OSLO

SCANDINAVIA, FINLAND AND ICELAND

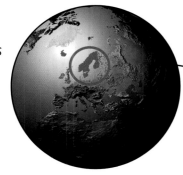

NORWEG SEA

S W

No spr

Drottningho Palace

L. Vänern

L. Vättern

Gothenburg

Little Mermaid

Legoland

Kalmar Castle

DENMARK COPENHAGEN

NORTH SEA

BA

GERMANY

Fact:

Hammerfest in Norw is the most northerly town in the world.

Maps like this show a country and its position in relation to the region in the main map.

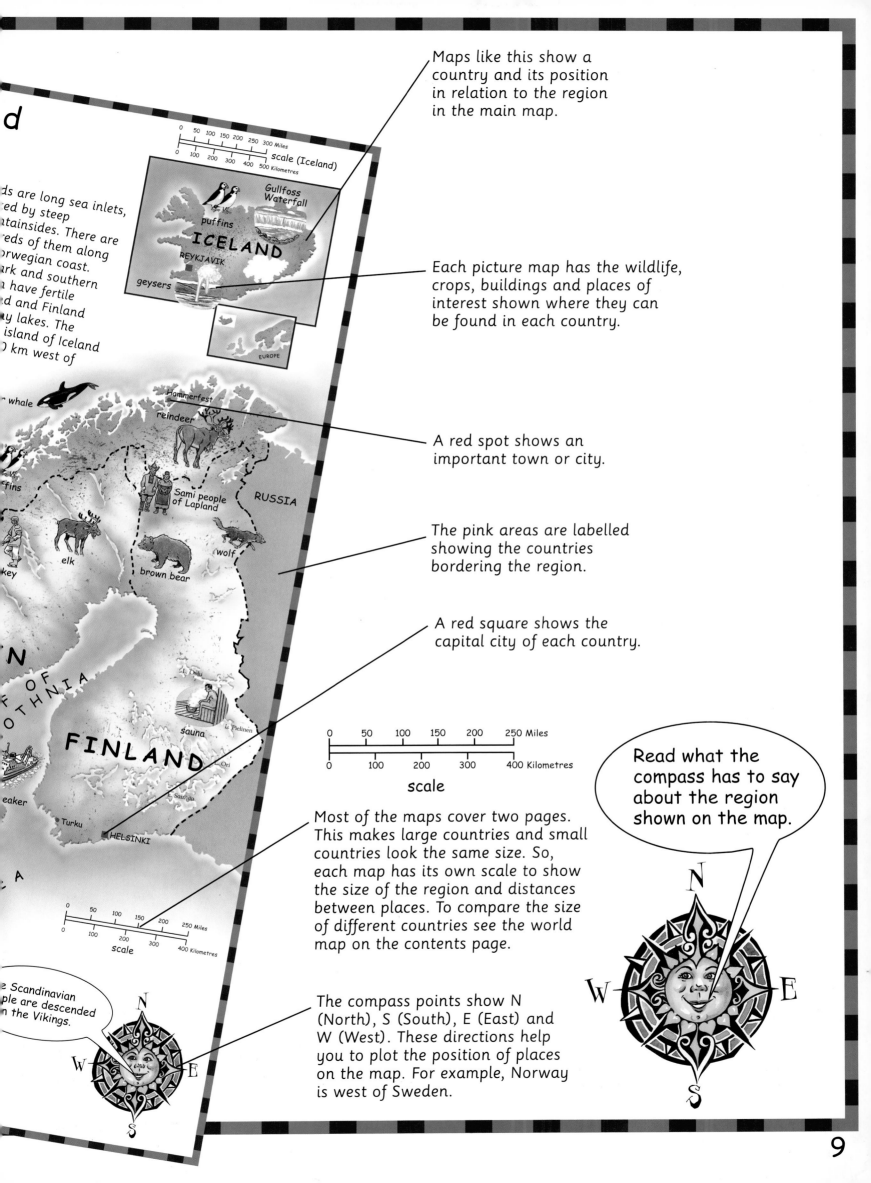

0 50 100 150 200 250 300 Miles
0 100 200 300 400 500 Kilometres
scale (Iceland)

ICELAND

Gullfoss Waterfall

puffins

REYKJAVIK

geysers

EUROPE

ds are long sea inlets,
ed by steep
tainsides. There are
eds of them along
orwegian coast.
ark and southern
a have fertile
d and Finland
y lakes. The
island of Iceland
) km west of

whale

Hammerfest

reindeer

Sami people of Lapland

RUSSIA

fins

elk

brown bear

wolf

key

N

F OF
OTHNIA

L. Oulu

sauna

L. Pielinen

FINLAND

L. Saimaa

eaker

Ori

Turku

HELSINKI

A

e Scandinavian
ple are descended
n the Vikings.

0 50 100 150 200 250 Miles
0 100 200 300 400 Kilometres
scale

N
W E
S

Each picture map has the wildlife, crops, buildings and places of interest shown where they can be found in each country.

A red spot shows an important town or city.

The pink areas are labelled showing the countries bordering the region.

A red square shows the capital city of each country.

0 50 100 150 200 250 Miles
0 100 200 300 400 Kilometres
scale

Most of the maps cover two pages. This makes large countries and small countries look the same size. So, each map has its own scale to show the size of the region and distances between places. To compare the size of different countries see the world map on the contents page.

The compass points show N (North), S (South), E (East) and W (West). These directions help you to plot the position of places on the map. For example, Norway is west of Sweden.

Read what the compass has to say about the region shown on the map.

N
W E
S

9

Canada and Greenland

Canada is the second biggest country in the world but it does not have a large population. Few people live in northern Canada as the climate there is too harsh.

Canada has two official languages: English and French. Montreal (above), in Quebec is the largest French-speaking city in the world after Paris.

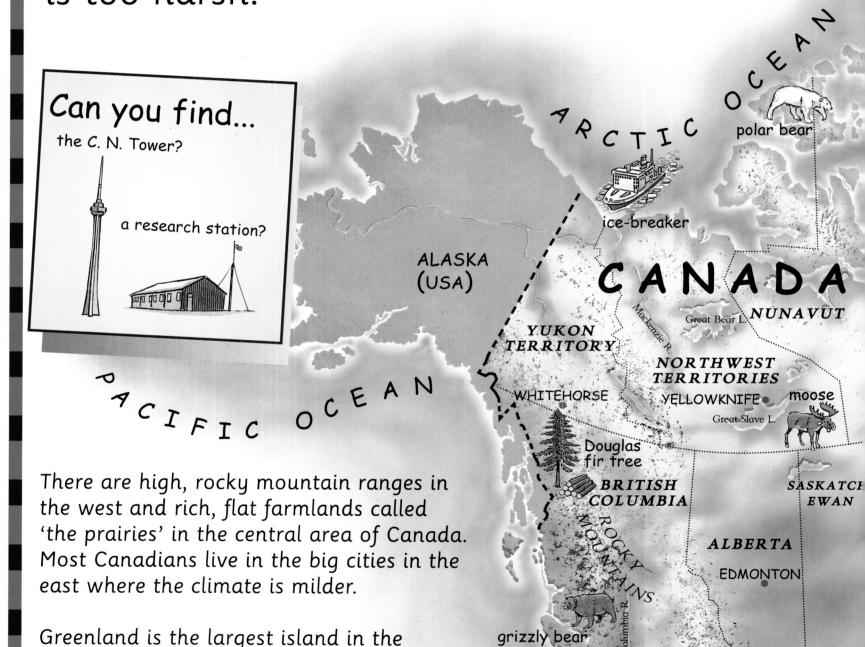

Can you find...

the C. N. Tower?

a research station?

There are high, rocky mountain ranges in the west and rich, flat farmlands called 'the prairies' in the central area of Canada. Most Canadians live in the big cities in the east where the climate is milder.

Greenland is the largest island in the world. It belongs to Denmark but has its own government. The Inuits who live in northern Canada and Greenland still hunt seals and polar bears.

ARCTIC OCEAN

polar bear

ice-breaker

ALASKA (USA)

PACIFIC OCEAN

CANADA

NUNAVUT

Mackenzie R.

Great Bear L.

YUKON TERRITORY

NORTHWEST TERRITORIES

WHITEHORSE

YELLOWKNIFE

Great Slave L.

moose

Douglas fir tree

BRITISH COLUMBIA

SASKATCH EWAN

ROCKY MOUNTAINS

Columbia R.

ALBERTA

EDMONTON

grizzly bear

REGIN

VICTORIA

Vancouver

UNITED STATES OF AMERICA

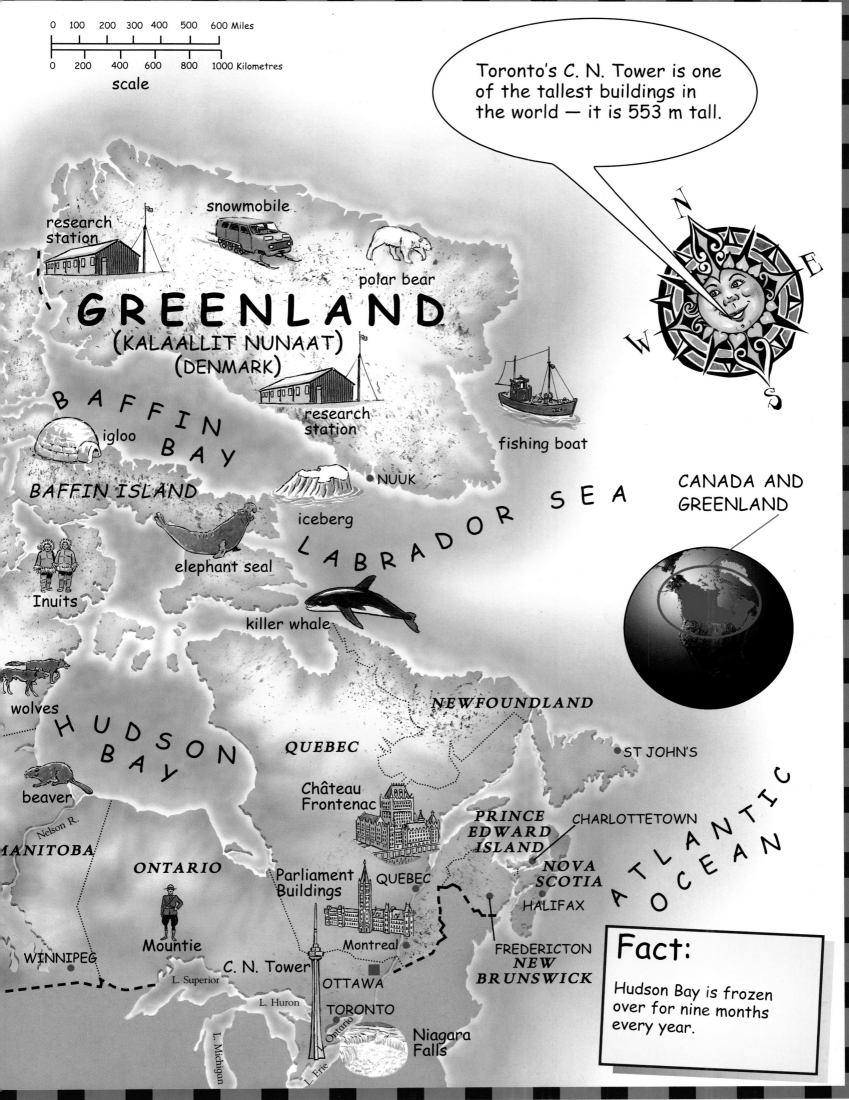

scale
0 100 200 300 400 500 600 Miles
0 200 400 600 800 1000 Kilometres

Toronto's C. N. Tower is one of the tallest buildings in the world — it is 553 m tall.

research station
snowmobile
polar bear

GREENLAND
(KALAALLIT NUNAAT)
(DENMARK)

BAFFIN BAY

igloo

research station

fishing boat

BAFFIN ISLAND

NUUK

iceberg

elephant seal

LABRADOR SEA

CANADA AND GREENLAND

Inuits

killer whale

wolves

HUDSON BAY

NEWFOUNDLAND

QUEBEC

ST JOHN'S

beaver

Nelson R.

Château Frontenac

PRINCE EDWARD ISLAND

CHARLOTTETOWN

MANITOBA

ONTARIO

Parliament Buildings

QUEBEC

NOVA SCOTIA

HALIFAX

ATLANTIC OCEAN

Mountie

WINNIPEG

C. N. Tower

L. Superior

Montreal

OTTAWA

FREDERICTON
NEW BRUNSWICK

Fact:

Hudson Bay is frozen over for nine months every year.

L. Huron

TORONTO

L. Michigan

L. Ontario

L. Erie

Niagara Falls

USA: The West and Midwest

The United States of America (USA) is one of the wealthiest countries in the world. It is made up of fifty states. The western states include Alaska in the far north and Hawaii, 4,000 km out in the Pacific Ocean.

The rugged landscape of the western states is dominated by the Rocky Mountains. California is the largest state in the region. More people live there than in any other American state.

PACIFIC OCEAN

Seattle
OLYMPIA
WASHINGTON

Columbia R.

Portland
SALEM

OREGON

redwood tree

BOISE

Golden Gate Bridge

NEVADA

Reno
CARSON CITY
SACRAMENTO

San Francisco

wild horses

CALIFORNIA

scale

0   100   200   300 Miles
0 100 200 300 400 500 Kilometres

grey whale

Las Vegas   L. Mead.

HOLLYWOOD

Los Angeles

San Diego

Colorado R.

PACIFIC OCEAN

walrus

caribou

ALASKA

Anchorage

whale

JUNEAU

0   200   400   600 Miles
0 200 400 600 800 1000 Kilometres

scale (Alaska)

NORTH AMERICA

N
W   E
S

Hamburgers were invented in the USA and are now eaten all over the world.

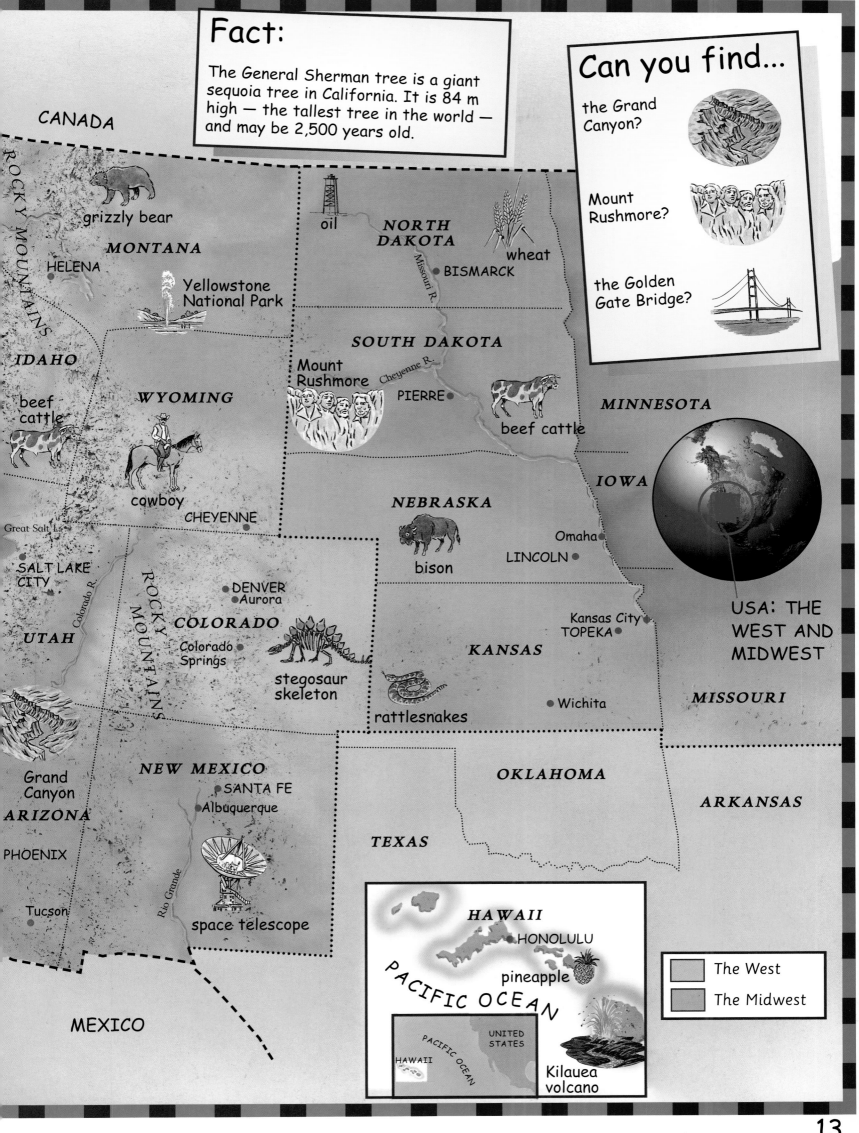

Fact:

The General Sherman tree is a giant sequoia tree in California. It is 84 m high — the tallest tree in the world — and may be 2,500 years old.

Can you find...

the Grand Canyon?

Mount Rushmore?

the Golden Gate Bridge?

CANADA

grizzly bear

oil

NORTH DAKOTA

wheat

MONTANA

HELENA

Missouri R.

BISMARCK

Yellowstone National Park

IDAHO

SOUTH DAKOTA

Mount Rushmore

Cheyenne R.

PIERRE

MINNESOTA

beef cattle

WYOMING

cowboy

CHEYENNE

IOWA

Great Salt L.

NEBRASKA

SALT LAKE CITY

bison

Omaha

LINCOLN

USA: THE WEST AND MIDWEST

Colorado R.

ROCKY MOUNTAINS

DENVER

Aurora

COLORADO

Colorado Springs

stegosaur skeleton

Kansas City

TOPEKA

UTAH

KANSAS

rattlesnakes

Wichita

MISSOURI

Grand Canyon

NEW MEXICO

SANTA FE

Albuquerque

OKLAHOMA

ARKANSAS

ARIZONA

PHOENIX

Rio Grande

TEXAS

Tucson

space telescope

HAWAII

HONOLULU

pineapple

PACIFIC OCEAN

PACIFIC OCEAN

UNITED STATES

HAWAII

Kilauea volcano

MEXICO

The West

The Midwest

USA: The Midwest and Northeast

The United States is the world's most industrial country. The area around the Great Lakes supplies most of the USA's iron and steel. Detroit is the centre of the American car industry.

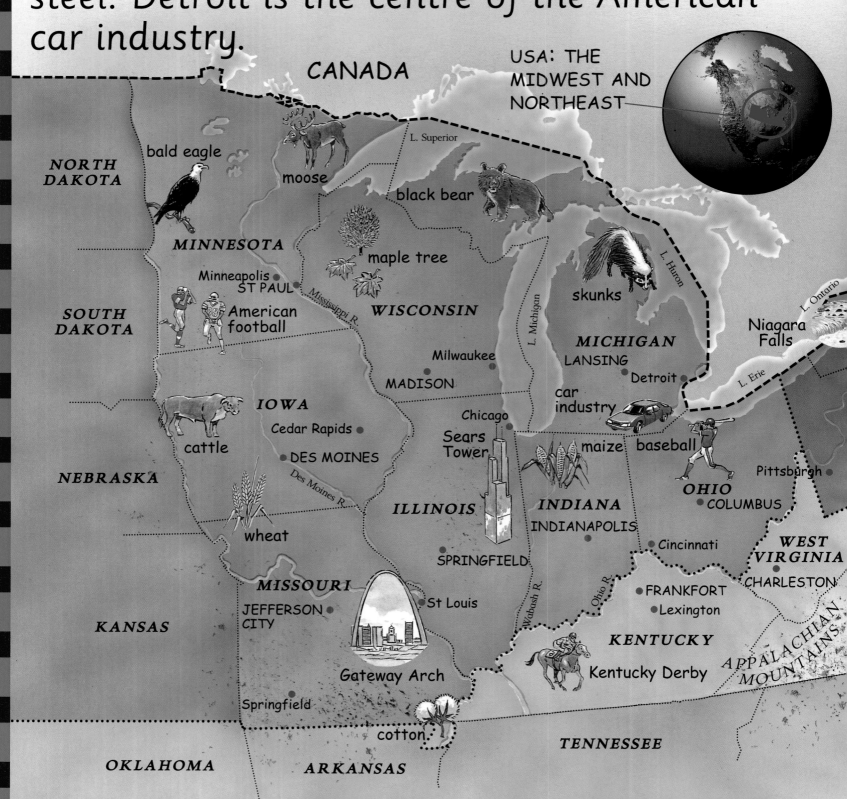

USA: THE MIDWEST AND NORTHEAST

CANADA

L. Superior

bald eagle

NORTH DAKOTA

moose

black bear

MINNESOTA

Minneapolis
ST PAUL

maple tree

L. Huron

skunks

L. Ontario

SOUTH DAKOTA

American football

Mississippi R.

WISCONSIN

L. Michigan

MICHIGAN
LANSING

Niagara Falls

Milwaukee

Detroit

MADISON

car industry

L. Erie

IOWA

Chicago

Cedar Rapids

Sears Tower

maize

baseball

cattle

DES MOINES

Pittsburgh

NEBRASKA

Des Moines R.

ILLINOIS

INDIANA

OHIO
COLUMBUS

wheat

INDIANAPOLIS

Cincinnati

WEST VIRGINIA

SPRINGFIELD

Wabash R.

Ohio R.

FRANKFORT

CHARLESTON

MISSOURI

St Louis

Lexington

JEFFERSON CITY

KANSAS

KENTUCKY

Kentucky Derby

APPALACHIAN MOUNTAINS

Gateway Arch

Springfield

cotton

TENNESSEE

OKLAHOMA

ARKANSAS

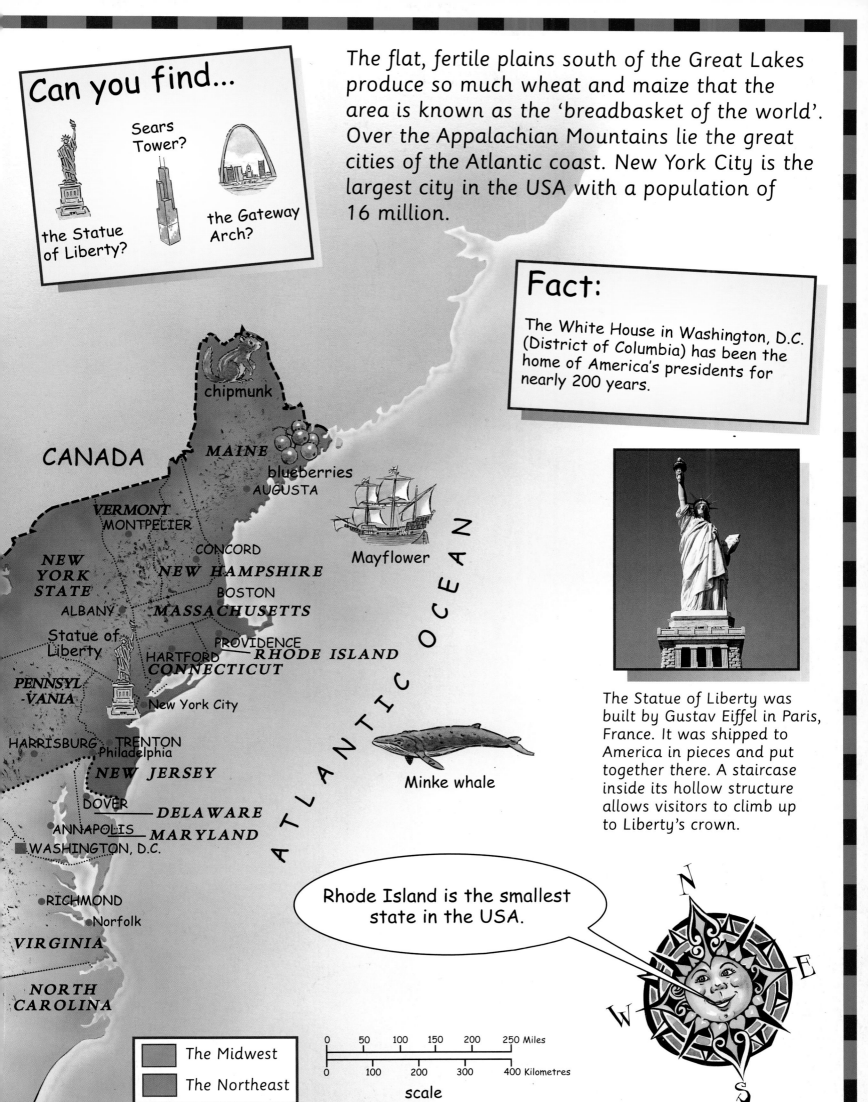

Can you find...

Sears Tower?

the Statue of Liberty?

the Gateway Arch?

The flat, fertile plains south of the Great Lakes produce so much wheat and maize that the area is known as the 'breadbasket of the world'. Over the Appalachian Mountains lie the great cities of the Atlantic coast. New York City is the largest city in the USA with a population of 16 million.

Fact:

The White House in Washington, D.C. (District of Columbia) has been the home of America's presidents for nearly 200 years.

chipmunk

CANADA

MAINE
blueberries
AUGUSTA

VERMONT
MONTPELIER

CONCORD

NEW YORK STATE

NEW HAMPSHIRE

BOSTON

ALBANY

MASSACHUSETTS

Statue of Liberty

PROVIDENCE
RHODE ISLAND

HARTFORD
CONNECTICUT

PENNSYL-VANIA

New York City

HARRISBURG
Philadelphia

TRENTON

NEW JERSEY

DOVER
DELAWARE

ANNAPOLIS
MARYLAND

WASHINGTON, D.C.

RICHMOND
Norfolk

VIRGINIA

NORTH CAROLINA

Mayflower

ATLANTIC OCEAN

Minke whale

The Statue of Liberty was built by Gustav Eiffel in Paris, France. It was shipped to America in pieces and put together there. A staircase inside its hollow structure allows visitors to climb up to Liberty's crown.

Rhode Island is the smallest state in the USA.

N

E

W

S

The Midwest

The Northeast

0   50   100   150   200   250 Miles
0   100   200   300   400 Kilometres
scale

USA: The South

USA: THE SOUTH

OKLAHOMA

• Tulsa

OKLAHOMA CITY

ARKANSAS

Arkansas R.

LITTLE RO

oil

• Amarillo

NEW MEXICO

Red R.

rodeo

TEXAS

Colorado R.

• Dallas

Brazos R.

El Paso

oil

cowboy

armadillo

longhorn cattle

Rio Grande R.

MEXICO

• AUSTIN

oil

Houston •

• San Antonio

San Antonio R.

Rio Grande R.

oil rig

Corpus Christi •

oil

The southern states extend to the Mexican border and include Texas, America's largest state. Texas is famous for its cattle ranches and oil wells.
The great Mississippi River runs through the South and flows into the Gulf of Mexico. Tobacco and cotton are grown in this region.

The Mississippi is one of the world's busiest rivers. Barges take cargo to the coast and tourists take paddle steamer trips.

N
W   E
S

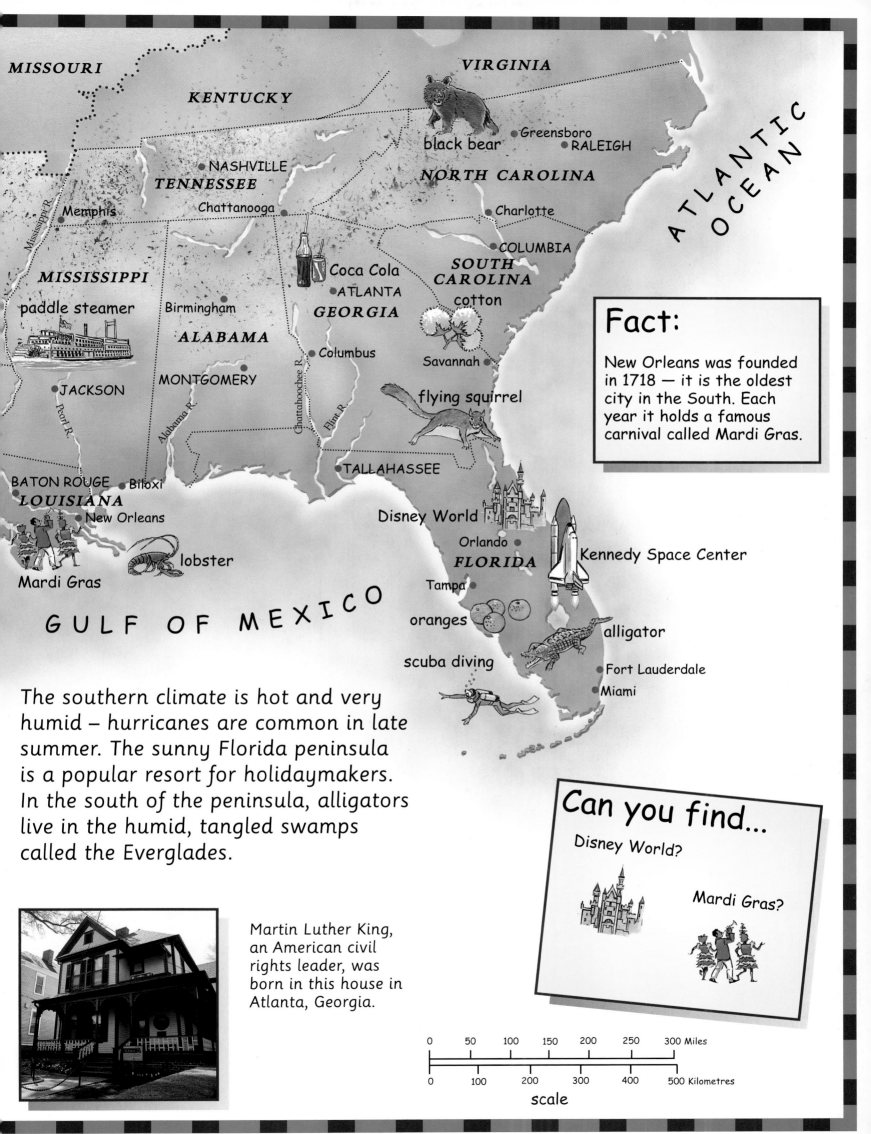

MISSOURI

KENTUCKY

VIRGINIA

black bear

Greensboro
• RALEIGH

NORTH CAROLINA

• NASHVILLE
TENNESSEE

Chattanooga

Charlotte

Memphis

• COLUMBIA
SOUTH
CAROLINA

Coca Cola

cotton

• ATLANTA

MISSISSIPPI

GEORGIA

paddle steamer

Birmingham

• Columbus

ALABAMA

Savannah

MONTGOMERY

flying squirrel

• JACKSON

• TALLAHASSEE

ATLANTIC OCEAN

Fact:

New Orleans was founded
in 1718 — it is the oldest
city in the South. Each
year it holds a famous
carnival called Mardi Gras.

BATON ROUGE   • Biloxi
LOUISIANA
• New Orleans

Disney World

lobster

Orlando •

Kennedy Space Center

Mardi Gras

FLORIDA

Tampa •

oranges

alligator

GULF OF MEXICO

scuba diving

Fort Lauderdale
• Miami

The southern climate is hot and very
humid — hurricanes are common in late
summer. The sunny Florida peninsula
is a popular resort for holidaymakers.
In the south of the peninsula, alligators
live in the humid, tangled swamps
called the Everglades.

Martin Luther King,
an American civil
rights leader, was
born in this house in
Atlanta, Georgia.

Can you find...

Disney World?

Mardi Gras?

0	50	100	150	200	250	300 Miles

0	100	200	300	400	500 Kilometres

scale

Mexico, Central America and the Caribbean

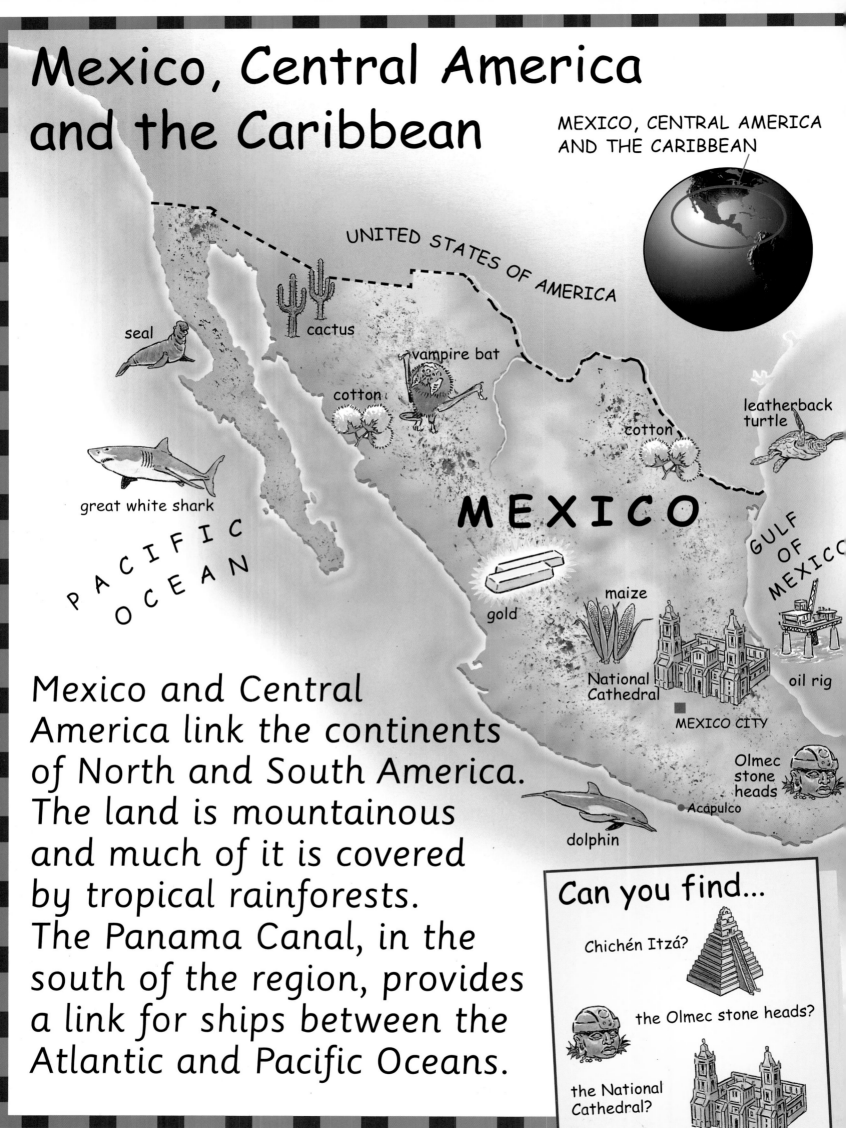

MEXICO, CENTRAL AMERICA AND THE CARIBBEAN

UNITED STATES OF AMERICA

seal

cactus

vampire bat

cotton

cotton

leatherback turtle

great white shark

PACIFIC OCEAN

MEXICO

gold

maize

National Cathedral

GULF OF MEXICO

oil rig

MEXICO CITY

Olmec stone heads

Acapulco

dolphin

Mexico and Central America link the continents of North and South America. The land is mountainous and much of it is covered by tropical rainforests. The Panama Canal, in the south of the region, provides a link for ships between the Atlantic and Pacific Oceans.

Can you find...

Chichén Itzá?

the Olmec stone heads?

the National Cathedral?

Mexico is this region's largest country. It is rich in silver and oil. Bananas and coffee grow in Central America and the Caribbean. The warm seas and climate of the Caribbean's volcanic islands attract many tourists.

This region is a hurricane zone. Fierce tropical storms sweep the Gulf of Mexico and the enormous waves they create cause a lot of damage.

CARIBBEAN ISLANDS

PUERTO RICO (US) SAN JUAN
BRITISH VIRGIN ISLANDS (UK)
ROAD TOWN
THE VALLEY
ANGUILLA (UK)
VIRGIN ISLANDS (US)
BASSETERRE
ANTIGUA AND BARBUDA
ST KITTS AND NEVIS
ST JOHNS
PLYMOUTH
GUADELOUPE (FRANCE)
MONTSERRAT (UK)
BASSE-TERRE
DOMINICA
ROSEAU
FORT-DE-FRANCE
MARTINIQUE
CASTRIES
ST LUCIA
ST VINCENT AND THE GRENADINES
BARBADOS
GRENADA
ST GEORGE'S
BRIDGETOWN
TRINIDAD AND TOBAGO
PORT OF SPAIN

ATLANTIC OCEAN
CUBA
SOUTH AMERICA

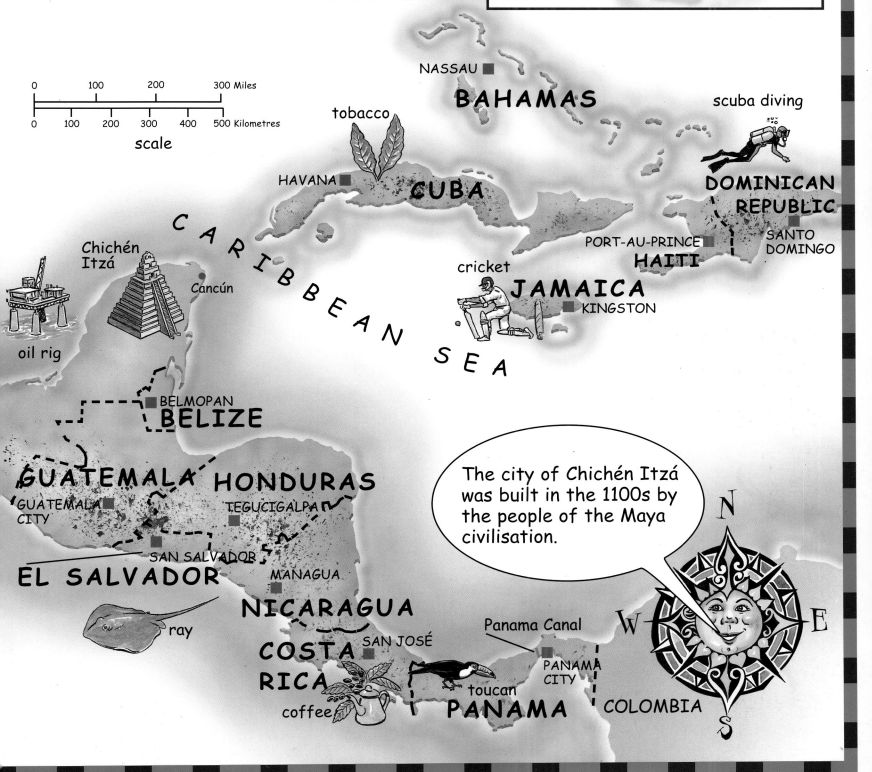

scale
0   100   200   300 Miles
0 100 200 300 400 500 Kilometres

NASSAU
BAHAMAS
scuba diving
tobacco
HAVANA
CUBA
DOMINICAN REPUBLIC
SANTO DOMINGO
PORT-AU-PRINCE
HAITI
cricket
JAMAICA
KINGSTON
C A R I B B E A N   S E A
Chichén Itzá
Cancún
oil rig
BELMOPAN
BELIZE
The city of Chichén Itzá was built in the 1100s by the people of the Maya civilisation.
GUATEMALA HONDURAS
GUATEMALA CITY
TEGUCIGALPA
SAN SALVADOR
EL SALVADOR
MANAGUA
NICARAGUA
ray
Panama Canal
COSTA RICA
SAN JOSÉ
PANAMA CITY
toucan
coffee
PANAMA
COLOMBIA
N
W   E
S

South America

Machu Picchu was a holy city, built by the Inca civilisation in the 15th century. The ancient mountain-top settlement in the Peruvian Andes was rediscovered in 1911.

SOUTH AMERICA

Tomatoes were first discovered growing in South America.

N
E
W
S

scale

0   100   200   300   400   500   600 Miles
0   200   400   600   800   1000 Kilometres

scale (Galapagos Islands)
30 Miles
0   25   50 Kilometres

A T L A N T I C   O C E A N

Natal

rainforest

BRAZIL

FRENCH GUIANA (FRANCE)

CAYENNE

SURINAME

PARAMARIBO

GUYANA

GEORGETOWN

Amazon R.

Xingu R.

piranha

Tapajos R.

anaconda

Ariane rocket launch site

Angel Falls

CARACAS

VENEZUELA

green turtle

jaguar

tarantula

Machu Picchu

COLOMBIA

BOGOTÁ

coffee

PANAMA

QUITO

EQUADOR

PERU

Ucayali R.

SOUTH AMERICA

GALAPAGOS ISLANDS (ECUADOR)

giant tortoise

marine iguana

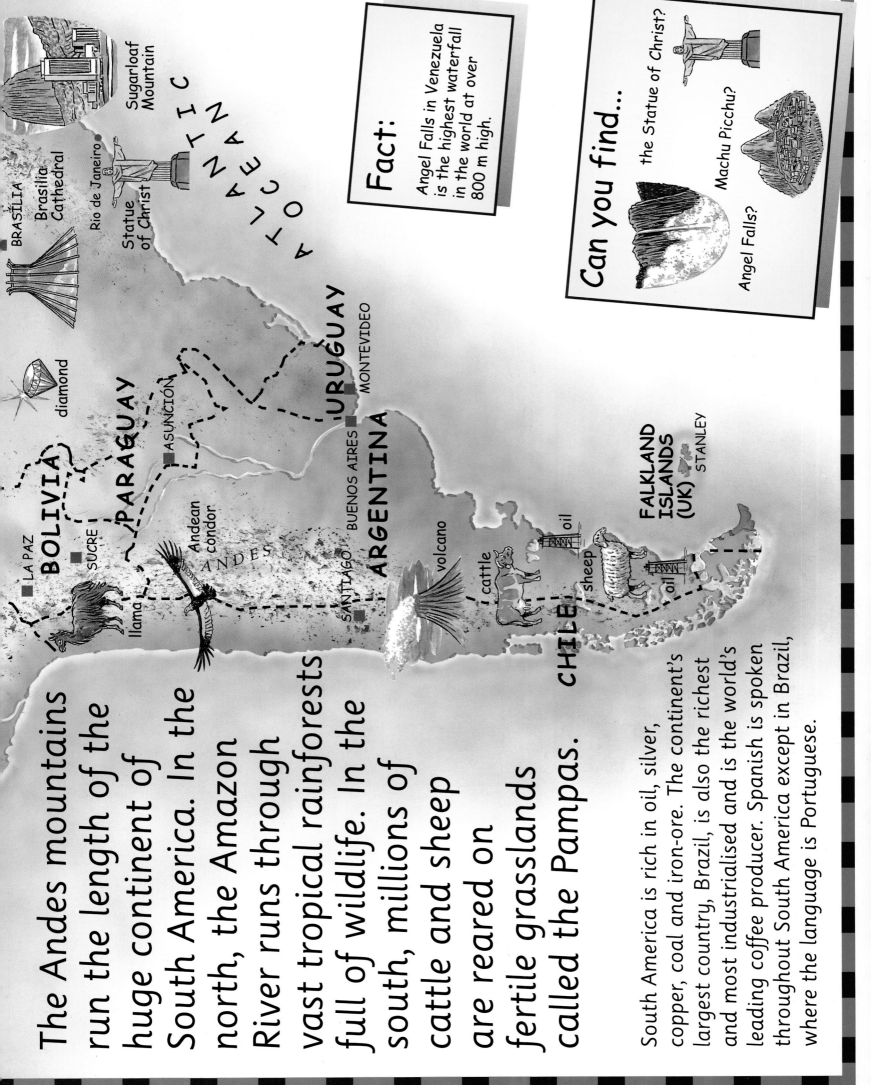

The Andes mountains run the length of the huge continent of South America. In the north, the Amazon River runs through vast tropical rainforests full of wildlife. In the south, millions of cattle and sheep are reared on fertile grasslands called the Pampas.

South America is rich in oil, silver, copper, coal and iron-ore. The continent's largest country, Brazil, is also the richest and most industrialised and is the world's leading coffee producer. Spanish is spoken throughout South America except in Brazil, where the language is Portuguese.

Fact:
Angel Falls in Venezuela is the highest waterfall in the world at over 800 m high.

Can you find...

the Statue of Christ?

Machu Picchu?

Angel Falls?

Map labels:

ATLANTIC OCEAN

BRASÍLIA
Brasília Cathedral
Sugarloaf Mountain
Rio de Janeiro
Statue of Christ

diamond

BOLIVIA
LA PAZ
SUCRE

PARAGUAY
ASUNCIÓN

URUGUAY
MONTEVIDEO

llama
Andean condor
ANDES

ARGENTINA
SANTIAGO
BUENOS AIRES

volcano
cattle

CHILE
sheep
oil

FALKLAND ISLANDS (UK)
STANLEY
oil

21

Scandinavia, Finland and Iceland

Norway, Sweden and Denmark are known as Scandinavia. These countries are rich in natural resources: timber, fish, oil and natural gas. They have warm summers but bitterly cold winters.

Fjords are long sea inlets, banked by steep mountainsides. There are hundreds of them along the Norwegian coast. Denmark and southern Sweden have fertile farmland and Finland has many lakes. The volcanic island of Iceland lies 1,000 km west of Norway.

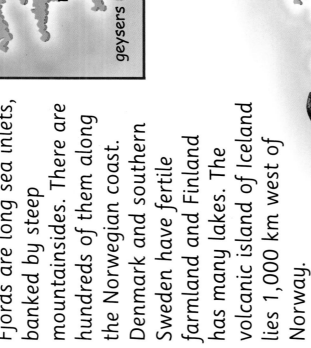

scale (Iceland)

0 50 100 150 200 250 300 Miles
0 100 200 300 400 500 Kilometres

Gullfoss Waterfall

puffins

ICELAND

REYKJAVIK

geysers

EUROPE

RUSSIA

wolf

brown bear

Sami people of Lapland

reindeer

Hammerfest

elk

ice hockey

puffins

killer whale

NORWEGIAN SEA

Can you find...

Legoland?

a stave church?

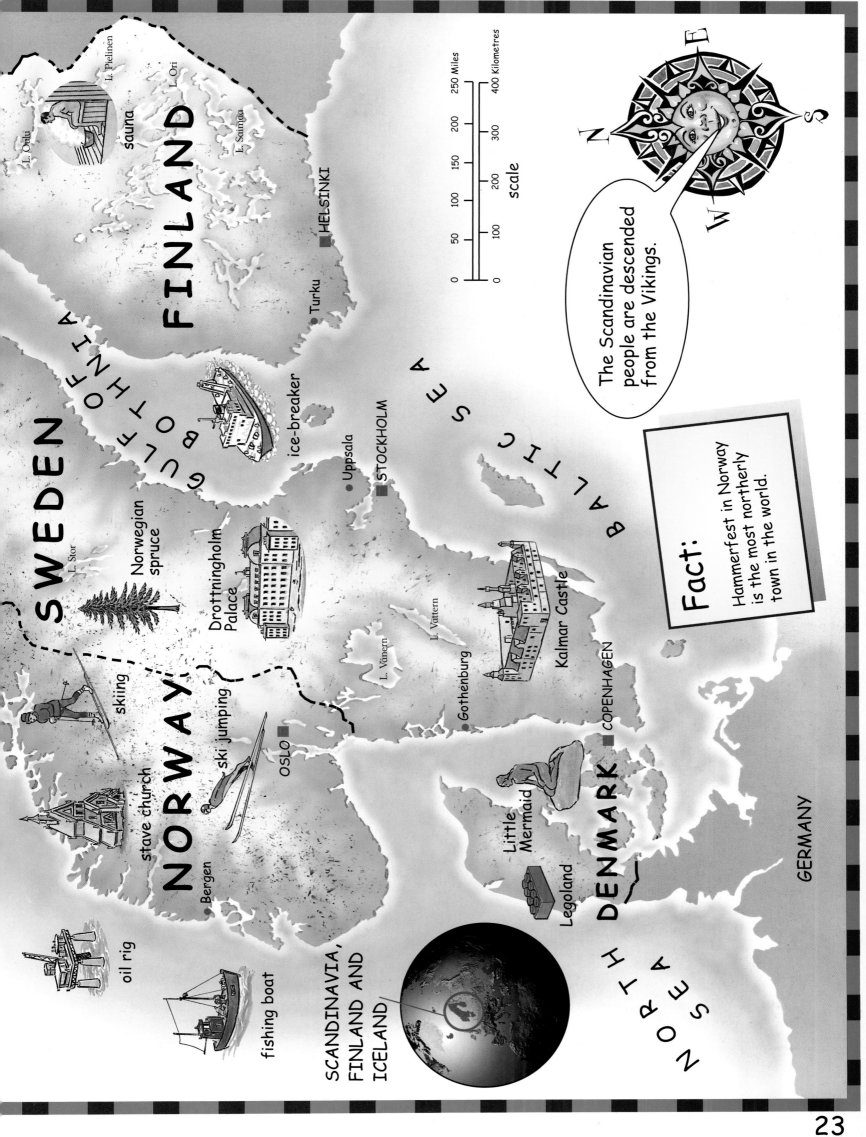

FINLAND

L. Oritu
L. Pielinen
L. Ori
L. Sainga

sauna

SWEDEN

L. Stor

GULF OF BOTHNIA

HELSINKI

Turku

ice-breaker

Norwegian spruce

Drottningholm Palace

Uppsala

STOCKHOLM

scale

250 Miles
400 Kilometres
200
300
150
200
100
100
50
0
0

The Scandinavian people are descended from the Vikings.

BALTIC SEA

skiing

stave church

Bergen

NORWAY

ski jumping

OSLO

L. Vänern

L. Vättern

Kalmar Castle

Gothenburg

COPENHAGEN

Little Mermaid

DENMARK

Legoland

GERMANY

oil rig

fishing boat

SCANDINAVIA, FINLAND AND ICELAND

NORTH SEA

Fact:
Hammerfest in Norway is the most northerly town in the world.

The British Isles

The United Kingdom (UK) and Ireland are known as the British Isles. Much of the land is farmed, but there are many large cities. London, the biggest city and the capital of the UK, is a major financial and cultural centre. The Channel Tunnel links the UK with mainland Europe.

Fact:

The Forth rail-bridge, Scotland, was the first major bridge in the world to be built of steel.

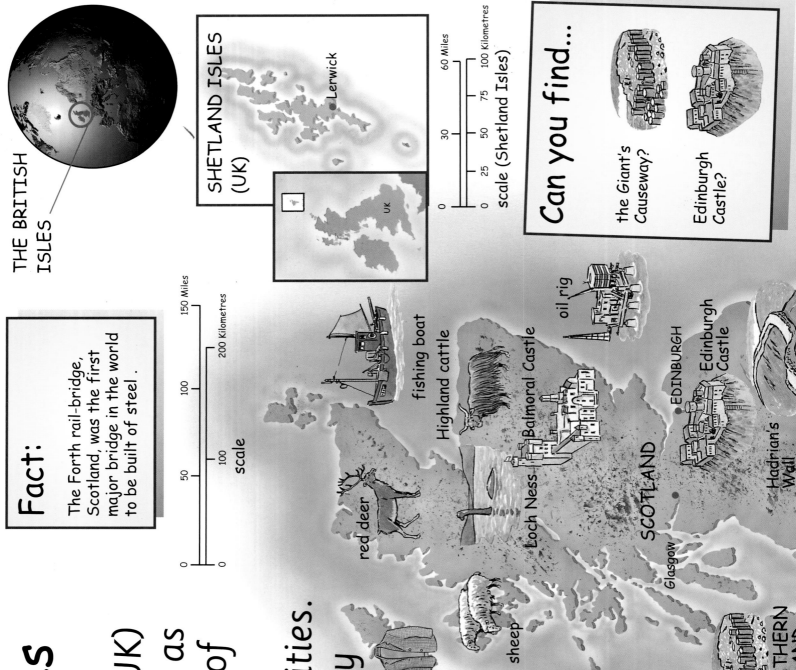

SHETLAND ISLES (UK)

Lerwick

scale (Shetland Isles)

0   25   50   75   100 Kilometres
0   30   60 Miles

UK

Can you find...

the Giant's Causeway?

Edinburgh Castle?

scale

0   50   100   150 Miles
0   100   200 Kilometres

red deer

Harris tweed

sheep

fishing boat

Highland cattle

oil rig

Balmoral Castle

Loch Ness

SCOTLAND

Glasgow

EDINBURGH

Edinburgh Castle

Hadrian's Wall

Giant's Causeway

NORTHERN IRELAND

ATLANTIC OCEAN

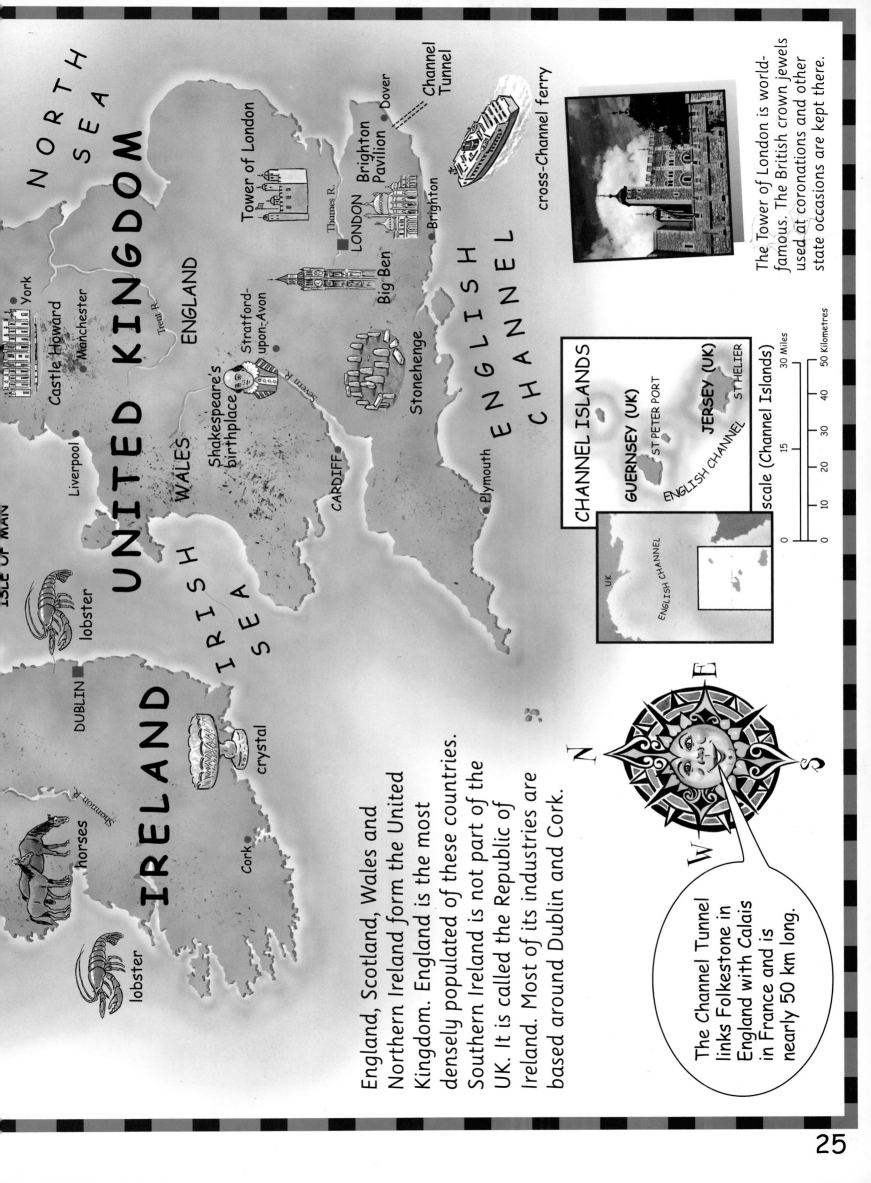

N O R T H   S E A

UNITED KINGDOM

ENGLAND

Tower of London

Channel Tunnel

Dover

Brighton Pavilion

LONDON

Thames R.

Big Ben

Brighton

cross-Channel ferry

Stratford-upon-Avon

Shakespeare's birthplace

Stonehenge

Severn R.

Trent R.

Castle Howard

Manchester

York

Liverpool

WALES

CARDIFF

Plymouth

ENGLISH CHANNEL

ISLE OF MAN

IRISH SEA

IRELAND

DUBLIN

crystal

Shannon R.

horses

Cork

lobster

lobster

The Tower of London is world-famous. The British crown jewels used at coronations and other state occasions are kept there.

CHANNEL ISLANDS

GUERNSEY (UK)

ST PETER PORT

JERSEY (UK)

ST HELIER

ENGLISH CHANNEL

scale (Channel Islands)

30 Miles

0   15

0   10   20   30   40   50 Kilometres

UK

ENGLISH CHANNEL

England, Scotland, Wales and Northern Ireland form the United Kingdom. England is the most densely populated of these countries. Southern Ireland is not part of the UK. It is called the Republic of Ireland. Most of its industries are based around Dublin and Cork.

N   E   S   W

The Channel Tunnel links Folkestone in England with Calais in France and is nearly 50 km long.

Spain and Portugal

SPAIN AND PORTUGAL

Madrid is the highest capital city in Europe at 640 m above sea level.

ATLANTIC OCEAN

Spain and Portugal form the Iberian Peninsula. They are separated from the rest of Europe by the Pyrenees mountains. Most of the peninsula is dry grassland with olive groves. This region is dry and hot in summer.

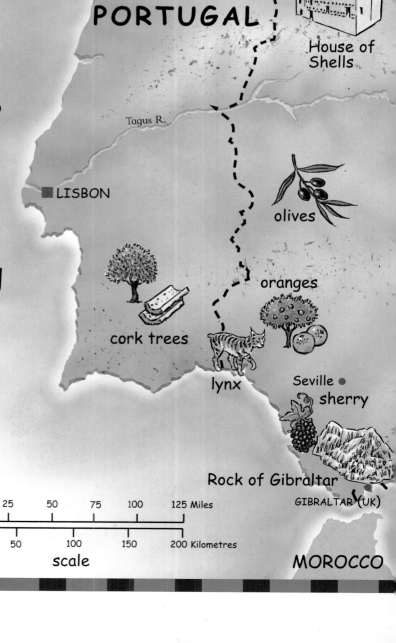

brown bear

maize

port

Oporto

PORTUGAL

House of Shells

Tagus R.

■LISBON

olives

oranges

cork trees

lynx

Seville ●

sherry

Rock of Gibraltar

GIBRALTAR (UK)

MOROCCO

Antonio Gaudi began work on Barcelona's famous church, the Sagrada Familia, in 1883. The building work still continues today because the church has not yet been completed.

| 0 | 25 | 50 | 75 | 100 | 125 Miles |
| 0 | 50 | 100 | 150 | 200 Kilometres |

scale

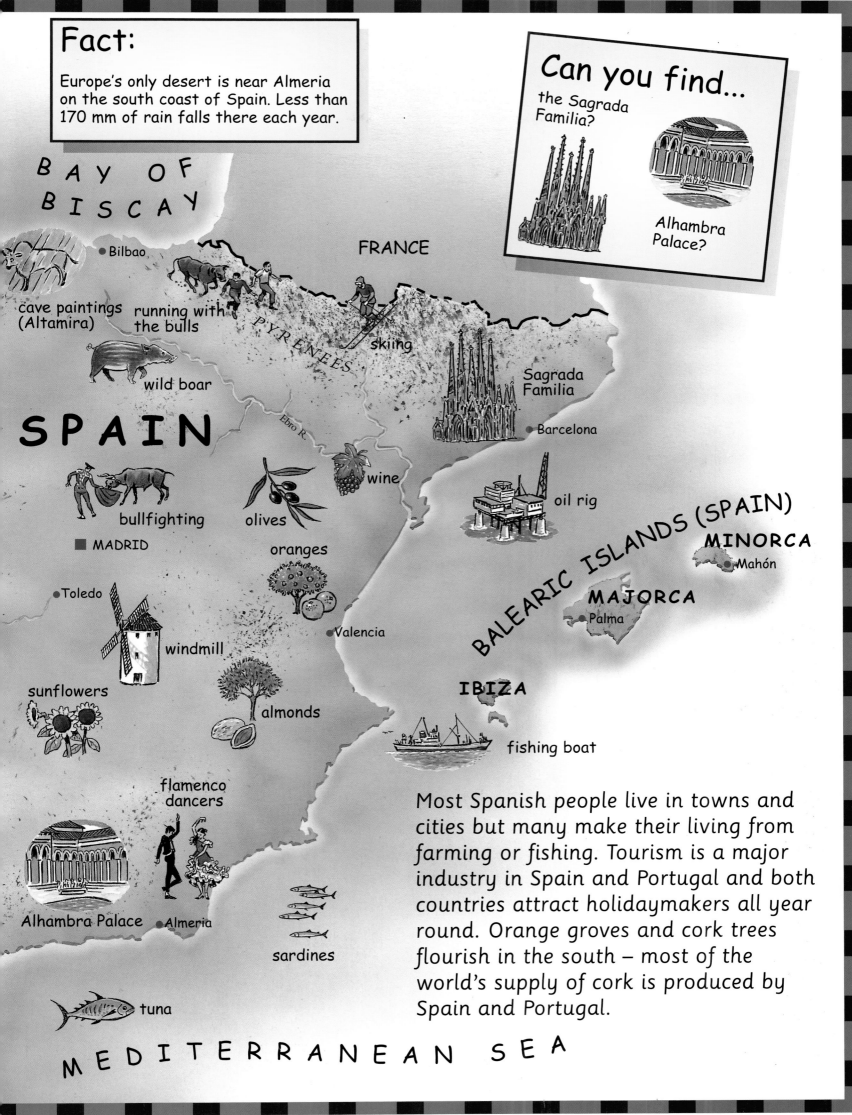

Fact:

Europe's only desert is near Almeria on the south coast of Spain. Less than 170 mm of rain falls there each year.

Can you find...

the Sagrada Familia?

Alhambra Palace?

BAY OF BISCAY

FRANCE

• Bilbao

cave paintings (Altamira)

running with the bulls

PYRENEES

skiing

wild boar

Sagrada Familia

SPAIN

Ebro R.

• Barcelona

bullfighting

olives

wine

oil rig

■ MADRID

oranges

BALEARIC ISLANDS (SPAIN)

MINORCA

• Mahón

MAJORCA

• Palma

• Toledo

windmill

• Valencia

sunflowers

almonds

IBIZA

fishing boat

flamenco dancers

Alhambra Palace

• Almeria

sardines

Most Spanish people live in towns and cities but many make their living from farming or fishing. Tourism is a major industry in Spain and Portugal and both countries attract holidaymakers all year round. Orange groves and cork trees flourish in the south – most of the world's supply of cork is produced by Spain and Portugal.

tuna

MEDITERRANEAN SEA

France

France is one of Europe's largest farming and industrial countries. Its mild climate becomes hotter and drier towards its southern borders with Italy and Spain. France is famous for its fine food and wines.

Can you find...

the Eiffel Tower?

Mont St. Michel?

the amphitheatre at Arles?

Much of France is farmland but most people now live in towns and cities.

The area around Paris, the capital city, is densely populated. Paris is famous for its great fashion houses, its smart restaurants and as a centre for the arts.

Andorra and Monaco are small, independent countries. Many wealthy people choose to live in Monaco because of its tax laws.

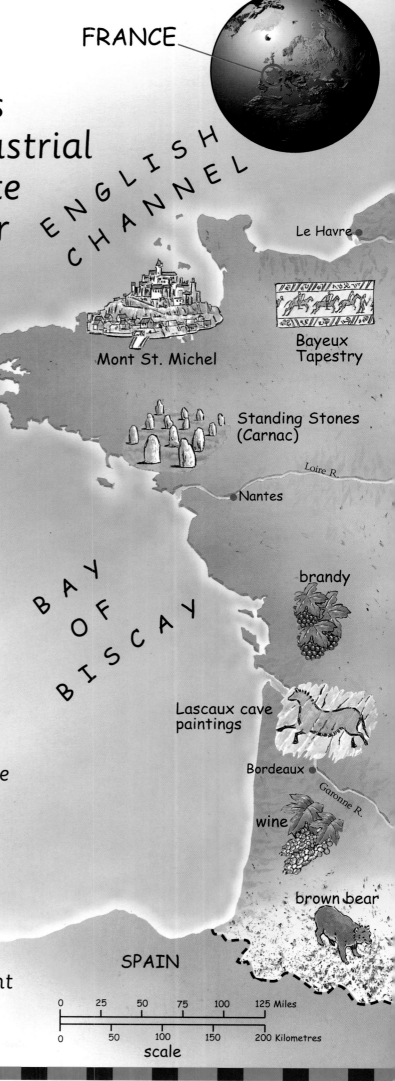

FRANCE

ENGLISH CHANNEL

Le Havre

Mont St. Michel

Bayeux Tapestry

Standing Stones (Carnac)

Loire R.

Nantes

BAY OF BISCAY

brandy

Lascaux cave paintings

Bordeaux

Garonne R.

wine

brown bear

SPAIN

| 0 | 25 | 50 | 75 | 100 | 125 Miles |

| 0 | 50 | 100 | 150 | 200 Kilometres |

scale

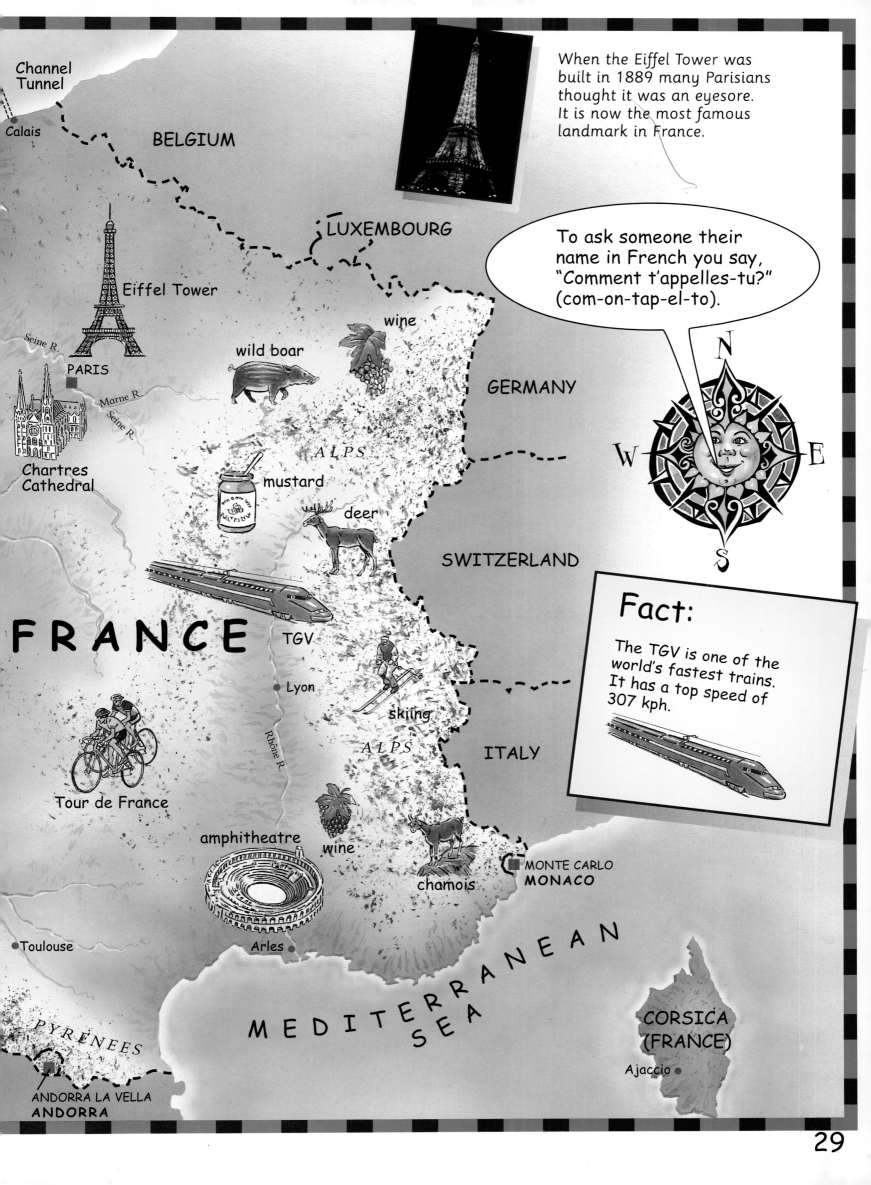

Channel Tunnel

Calais

BELGIUM

When the Eiffel Tower was built in 1889 many Parisians thought it was an eyesore. It is now the most famous landmark in France.

LUXEMBOURG

Eiffel Tower

wine

wild boar

To ask someone their name in French you say, "Comment t'appelles-tu?" (com-on-tap-el-to).

Seine R.

PARIS

Marne R.

Seine R.

GERMANY

N

W   E

S

Chartres Cathedral

ALPS

mustard

deer

SWITZERLAND

FRANCE

TGV

Lyon

Fact:

The TGV is one of the world's fastest trains. It has a top speed of 307 kph.

Rhône R.

skiing

ALPS

ITALY

Tour de France

amphitheatre

wine

chamois

MONTE CARLO
MONACO

Toulouse

Arles

M E D I T E R R A N E A N

S E A

CORSICA (FRANCE)

Ajaccio

PYRENEES

ANDORRA LA VELLA
ANDORRA

Belgium, the Netherlands and Luxembourg

This part of Europe is called 'the Low Countries'. Most of the land in these countries is flat. Large areas of land have been reclaimed from the sea by draining it and building long dykes (walls) to protect the land from flooding.

Belgium is famous for lacemaking and fine chocolate.

N
W — E
S

BELGIUM, THE NETHERLANDS AND LUXEMBOURG

windmill

clogs

seal

ice skating

THE NETHERLANDS

GERMANY

Ijssel R.

AMSTERDAM

canal house

Delft pottery

Edam cheese

diamond cutting

tulips

Rotterdam

Lek R.

The Hague

NORTH SEA

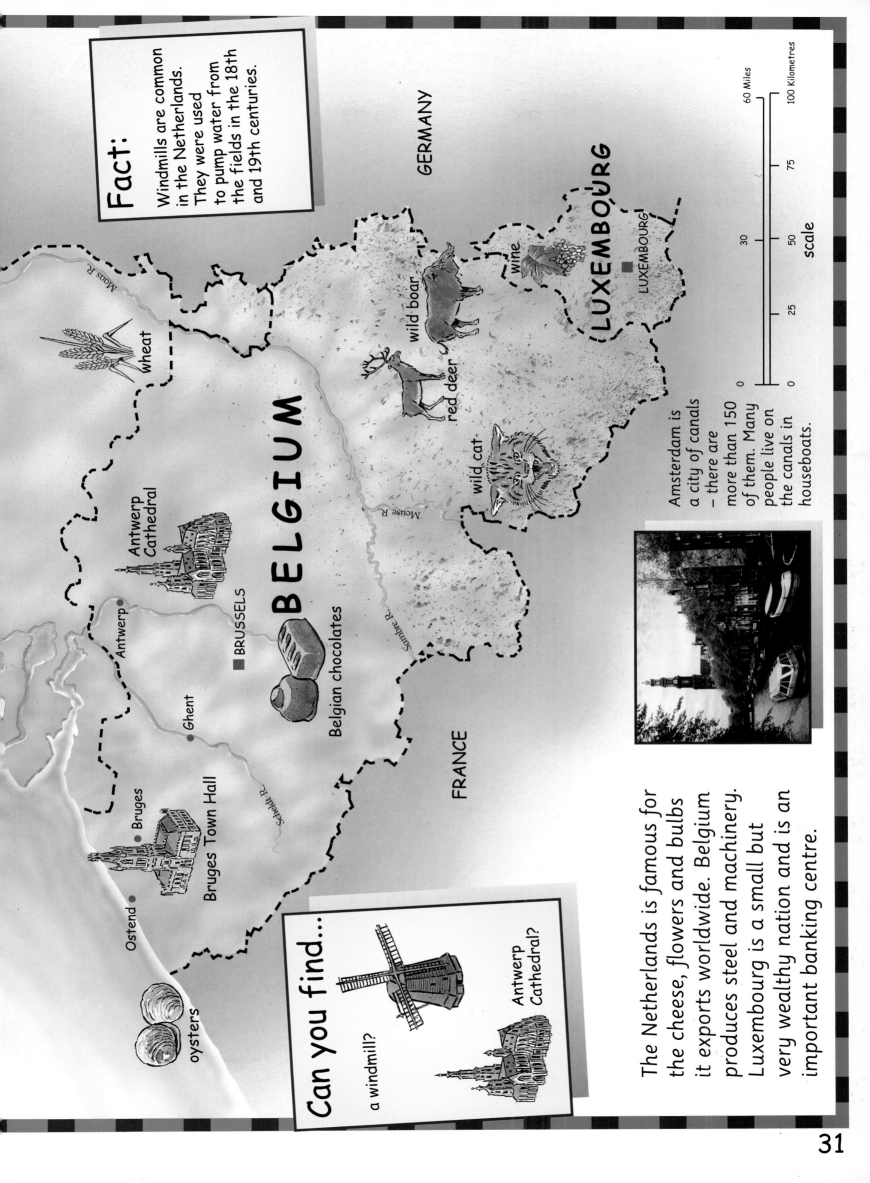

GERMANY

LUXEMBOURG

60 Miles

100 Kilometres

0   25   50   75   100

scale

0   30

wine

wild boar

red deer

Meuse R.

wild cat

LUXEMBOURG

Maas R.

wheat

BELGIUM

Antwerp Cathedral

Antwerp

■ BRUSSELS

Ghent

Schelde R.

Bruges

Ostend

oysters

Bruges Town Hall

Belgian chocolates

Sambre R.

FRANCE

Amsterdam is a city of canals – there are more than 150 of them. Many people live on the canals in houseboats.

Can you find...

a windmill?

Antwerp Cathedral?

The Netherlands is famous for the cheese, flowers and bulbs it exports worldwide. Belgium produces steel and machinery. Luxembourg is a small but very wealthy nation and is an important banking centre.

Neuschwanstein Castle was built by King Louis II. Walt Disney based his fairy-tale castle on this fantastic building.

GERMANY, AUSTRIA AND SWITZERLAND

Germany, Austria and Switzerland

Germany is a wealthy industrial nation. It produces cars, electrical goods, wines and beers. It has a large population and many large cities. There are forests, long rivers and lots of fine castles. Germany's large rivers are important for transporting goods around the country.

NORTH SEA

NETHERLANDS

Weser R.

sausages

Rhine R.

Cologne Cathedral

Düsseldorf

Cologne

Bonn

Beethoven's birthplace

BELGIUM

LUXEMBOURG

Roman ruins

FRANCE

cuckoo clock

wine

Zurich

watch

Gruyère cheese

BERNE

SWITZERLAND

L. Geneva

chocolates

scale

0	25	50	75	100	125 Miles
0	50	100	150	200 Kilometres	

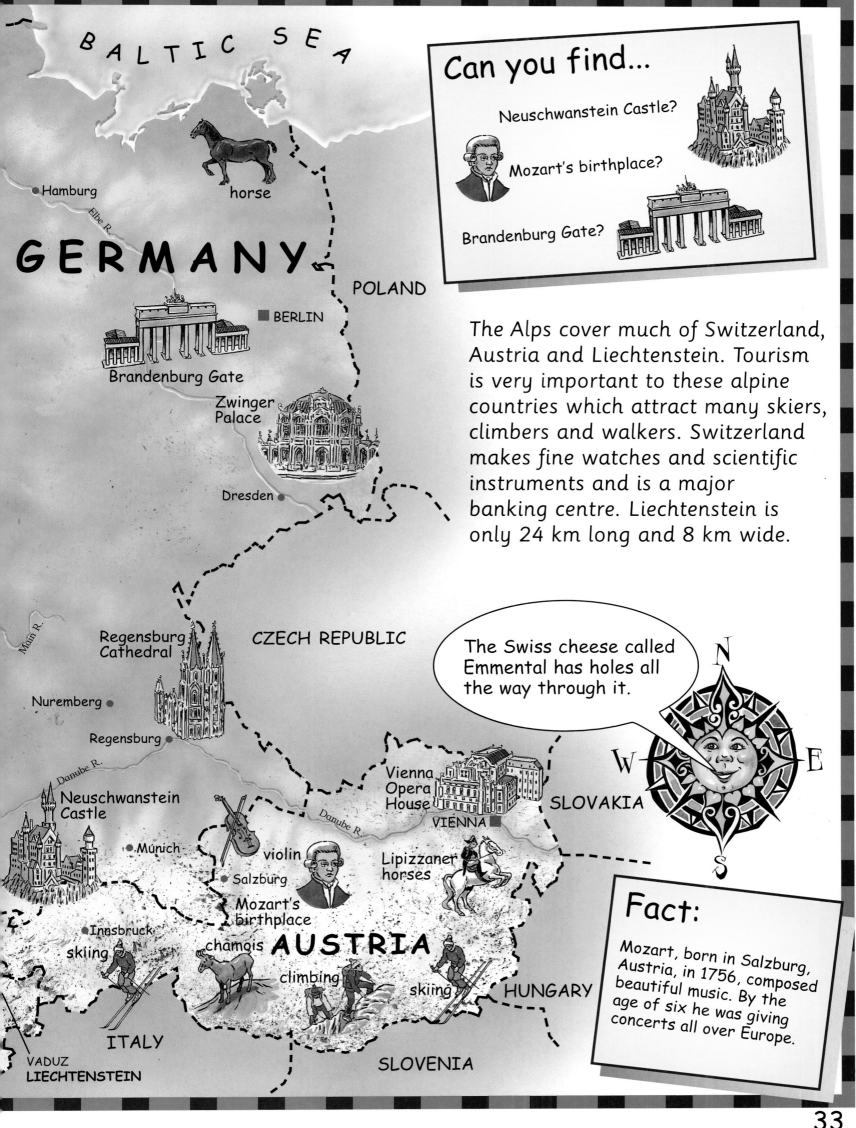

BALTIC SEA

GERMANY

Hamburg

Elbe R.

horse

Can you find...

Neuschwanstein Castle?

Mozart's birthplace?

Brandenburg Gate?

POLAND

BERLIN

Brandenburg Gate

Zwinger Palace

Dresden

The Alps cover much of Switzerland, Austria and Liechtenstein. Tourism is very important to these alpine countries which attract many skiers, climbers and walkers. Switzerland makes fine watches and scientific instruments and is a major banking centre. Liechtenstein is only 24 km long and 8 km wide.

Main R.

Regensburg Cathedral

CZECH REPUBLIC

The Swiss cheese called Emmental has holes all the way through it.

Nuremberg

Regensburg

Danube R.

Neuschwanstein Castle

Vienna Opera House

SLOVAKIA

N

W   E

S

Munich

violin

Salzburg

Mozart's birthplace

Lipizzaner horses

VIENNA

Danube R.

Fact:

Innsbruck

chamois AUSTRIA

Mozart, born in Salzburg, Austria, in 1756, composed beautiful music. By the age of six he was giving concerts all over Europe.

skiing

climbing

skiing

HUNGARY

ITALY

VADUZ
LIECHTENSTEIN

SLOVENIA

33

Italy and Malta

Italy is famous for its art, food, fashion and cars. Most of its population, industry and farmland are concentrated along the River Po in the north.

Can you find...

Pompeii? the Leaning Tower of Pisa? the Colosseum?

Fact:

Pizza is a traditional food that was invented in Italy. It is now eaten worldwide.

scale

25 50 75 100 125 Miles

0   50 100 150 200 Kilometres

AUSTRIA

SLOVENIA

CROATIA

SWITZERLAND

ALPS

St Mark's Square

Milan Cathedral

• Milan

violin

L. Garda

Parmesan cheese

Po R.

gondolier

Venice

pasta

Parma ham

Leaning Tower of Pisa

Florence Cathedral

• Pisa

• Florence

ITALY

SAN MARINO
SAN MARINO

Tiber R.

Colosseum

ROME
VATICAN CITY

Vatican

ALPS

FRANCE

Turin

wine

olives

LIGURIAN SEA

CORSICA (FRANCE)

ADRIATIC SEA

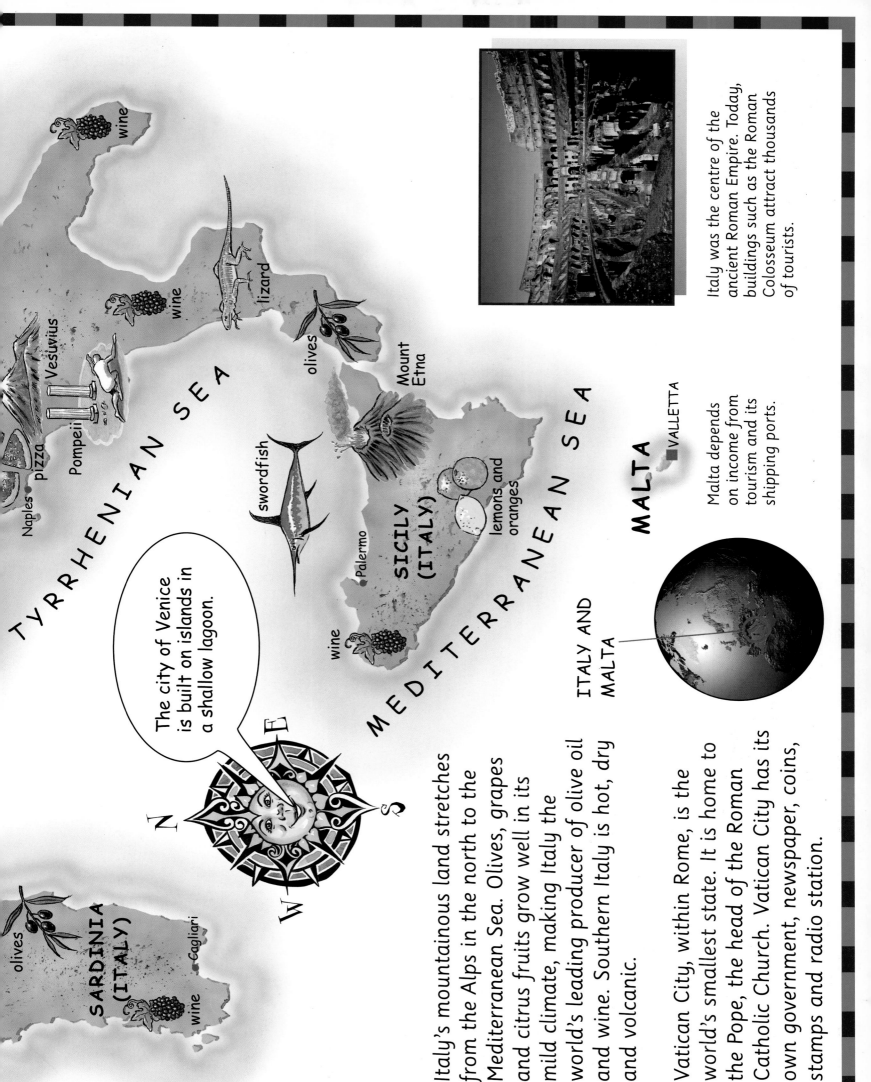

wine

wine

Vesuvius

Pompeii

Naples • pizza

lizard

olives

Mount Etna

swordfish

T Y R R H E N I A N   S E A

The city of Venice is built on islands in a shallow lagoon.

Palermo •

SICILY (ITALY)

lemons and oranges

wine

M E D I T E R R A N E A N   S E A

MALTA

■ VALLETTA

Malta depends on income from tourism and its shipping ports.

ITALY AND MALTA

olives

SARDINIA (ITALY)

wine

Cagliari

N E S W

Italy's mountainous land stretches from the Alps in the north to the Mediterranean Sea. Olives, grapes and citrus fruits grow well in its mild climate, making Italy the world's leading producer of olive oil and wine. Southern Italy is hot, dry and volcanic.

Vatican City, within Rome, is the world's smallest state. It is home to the Pope, the head of the Roman Catholic Church. Vatican City has its own government, newspaper, coins, stamps and radio station.

Italy was the centre of the ancient Roman Empire. Today, buildings such as the Roman Colosseum attract thousands of tourists.

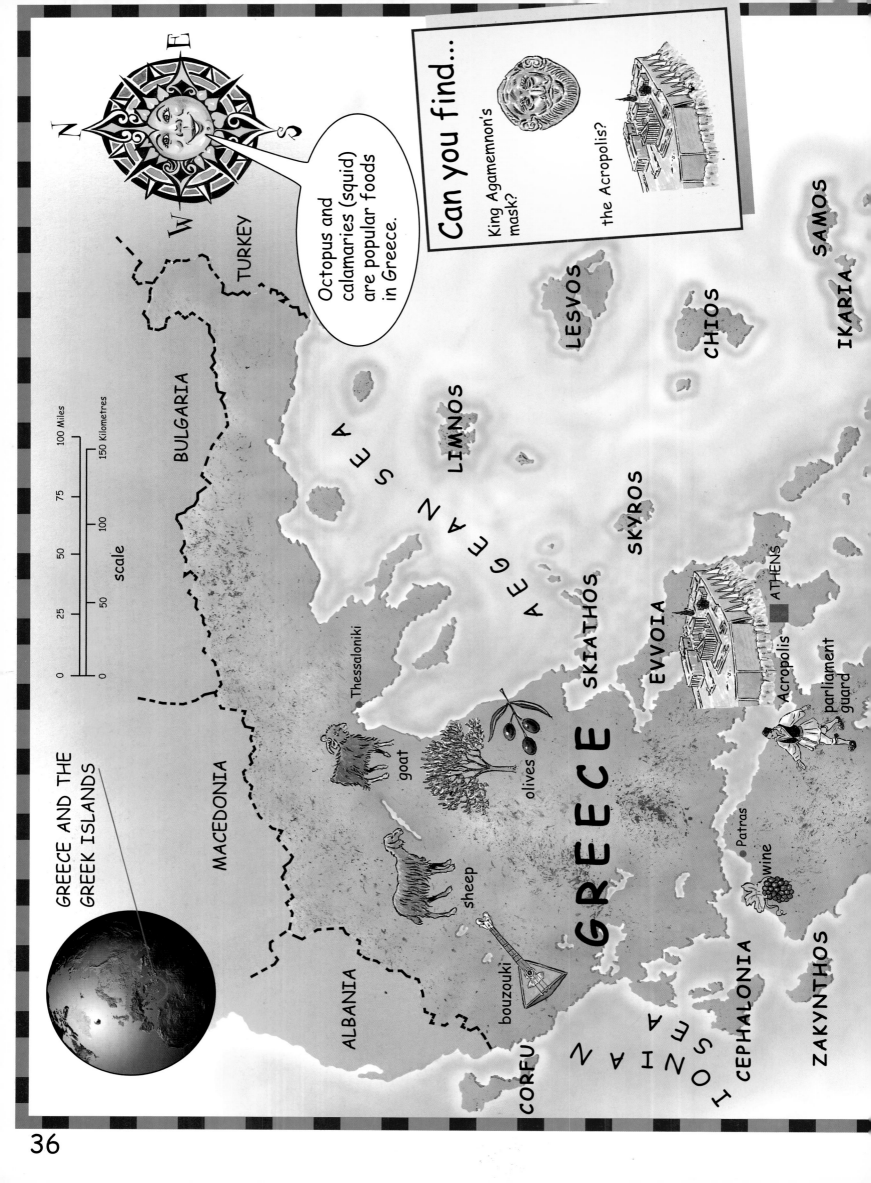

GREECE AND THE GREEK ISLANDS

Octopus and calamaries (squid) are popular foods in Greece.

Can you find...

King Agamemnon's mask?

the Acropolis?

N E W S

scale

0   25   50   75   100 Miles

0   50   100   150 Kilometres

TURKEY

BULGARIA

MACEDONIA

ALBANIA

Thessaloniki

AEGEAN SEA

LIMNOS

LESVOS

CHIOS

SAMOS

IKARIA

SKYROS

SKIATHOS

EVVOIA

ATHENS

Acropolis

parliament guard

goat

olives

sheep

bouzouki

GREECE

Patras

wine

CORFU

CEPHALONIA

ZAKYNTHOS

IONIAN SEA

36

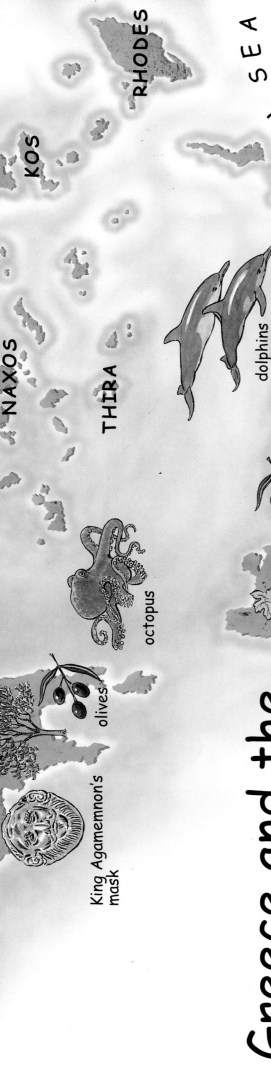

Greece and the Greek Islands

Greece is in southern Europe. It is a dry, mountainous country with many islands. The capital city, Athens, is home to more than one third of Greece's population. Farming and tourism are the major industries.

The Ancient Greeks were Europe's first great civilisation. Each year, thousands of tourists explore Greece's ancient buildings and archaeological sites. Greece is a popular holiday destination, attracting many visitors with its scenery, sunshine and fine beaches. Its hot climate is ideal for growing olives, grapes and citrus fruits.

The Parthenon is an ancient Greek temple. It stands on the Acropolis – a rocky hill that towers over the city of Athens.

King Agamemnon's mask

olives

octopus

dolphins

NAXOS

THIRA

KOS

RHODES

wine

olives

CRETE

• Irá Klion

MEDITERRANEAN SEA

The south of the region is rugged and mountainous with many areas of rich farmland. In 1993 Czechoslovakia split into two countries: the Czech Republic and Slovakia. Slovenia, Bosnia and Herzegovina, Croatia, and Macedonia were all once part of Yugoslavia, but have recently become independent countries.

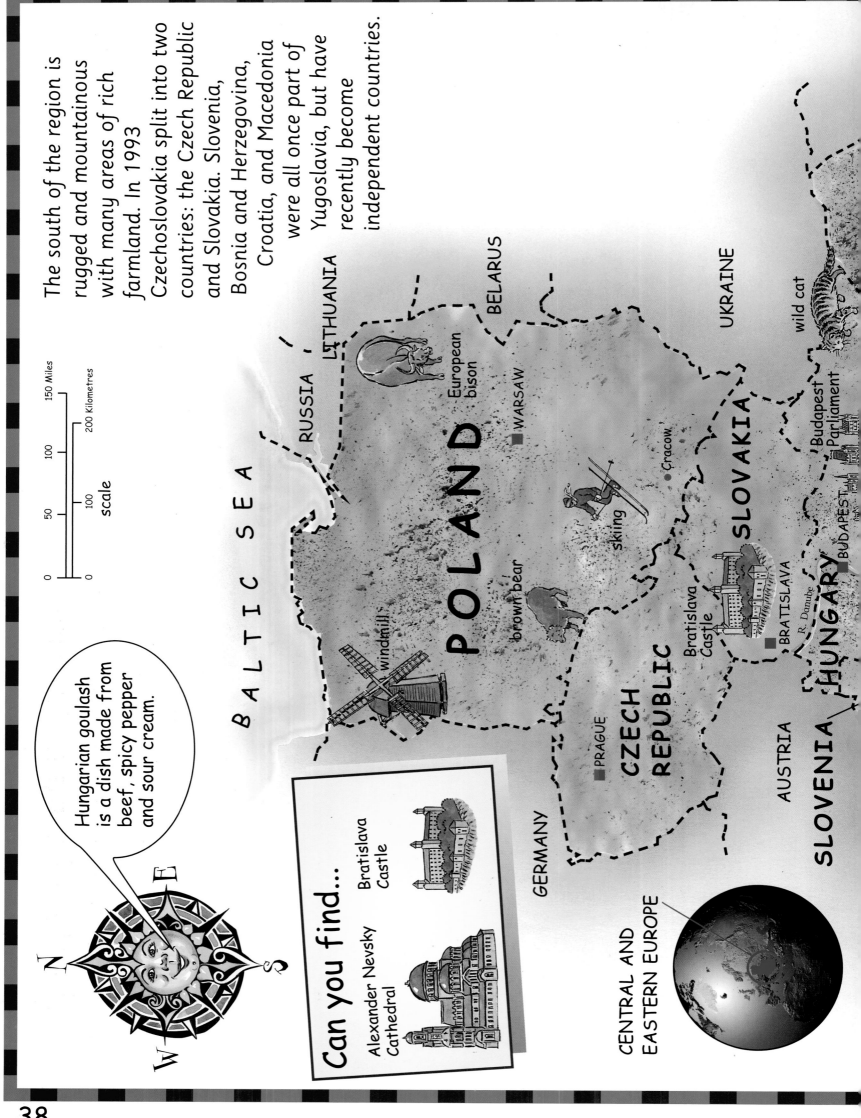

Hungarian goulash is a dish made from beef, spicy pepper and sour cream.

N E W S

Can you find...

Bratislava Castle

Alexander Nevsky Cathedral

BALTIC SEA

RUSSIA

LITHUANIA

BELARUS

UKRAINE

POLAND

European bison

WARSAW

Cracow

skiing

brown bear

windmill

CZECH REPUBLIC

PRAGUE

GERMANY

SLOVAKIA

Bratislava Castle

BRATISLAVA

R. Danube

AUSTRIA

SLOVENIA

HUNGARY

BUDAPEST

Budapest Parliament

wild cat

CENTRAL AND EASTERN EUROPE

scale

150 Miles

200 Kilometres

100

50

100

0

0

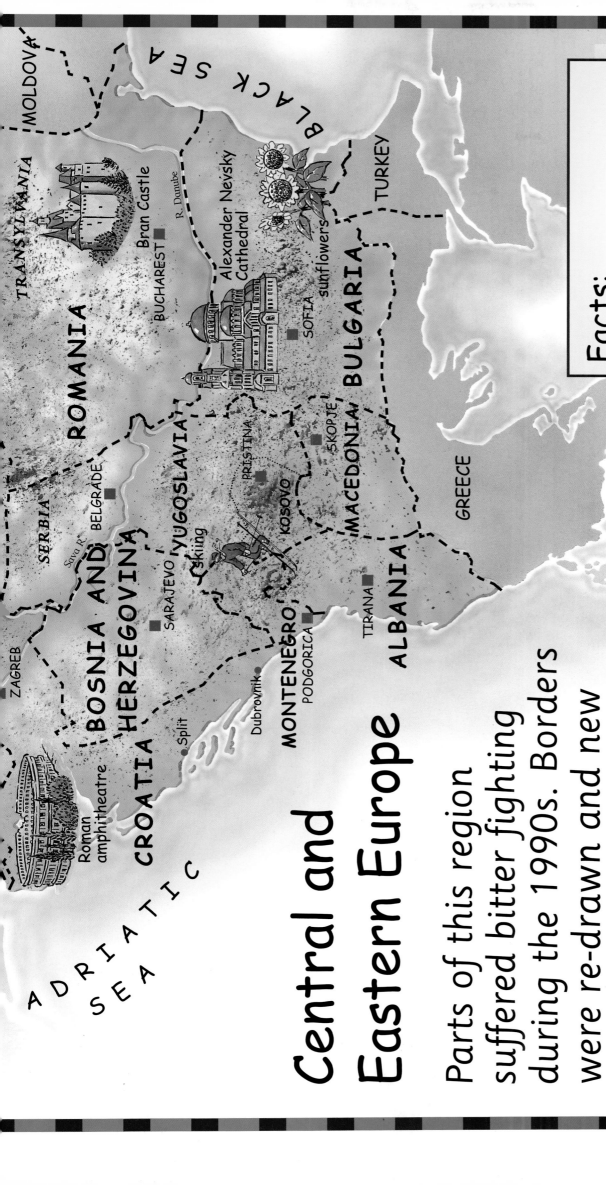

Central and Eastern Europe

Parts of this region suffered bitter fighting during the 1990s. Borders were re-drawn and new countries have been created. Poland, the largest and most populated country in the region, has major iron, steel and shipbuilding industries.

Map labels:
- MOLDOVA
- BLACK SEA
- TRANSYLVANIA
- Bran Castle
- R. Danube
- ROMANIA
- BUCHAREST
- Alexander Nevsky Cathedral
- sunflowers
- TURKEY
- SOFIA
- BULGARIA
- SERBIA
- BELGRADE
- Sava R.
- YUGOSLAVIA
- PRISTINA
- KOSOVO
- SKOPJE
- MACEDONIA
- BOSNIA AND HERZEGOVINA
- SARAJEVO
- skiing
- GREECE
- ZAGREB
- CROATIA
- Split
- Dubrovnik
- Roman amphitheatre
- MONTENEGRO
- PODGORICA
- TIRANA
- ALBANIA
- ADRIATIC SEA

Facts:

- Heavy industry has caused serious pollution problems in Poland, Hungary and the Czech Republic.

- Budapest, the capital city of Hungary, was once two towns separated by the River Danube. One town was called Buda and the other Pest.

Northern Eurasia

This vast region stretches across Asia and Europe. Until 1991 it was one single country, the Soviet Union. Today, it is made up of 15 independent nations including Russia, the largest country in the world.

NORTHERN EURASIA

BARENTS SEA

polar bear

ice-breaker

FINLAND

Winter Palace

TALLIN

ESTONIA

Kremlin

LATVIA

RIGA

LITHUANIA

VILNIUS

POLAND

MINSK

BELARUS

MOSCOW

St. Basil's Cathedral

RUSSIA

URAL MOUNTAINS

oil

woolly mammoth fossils

Fabergé egg

balalaika

Yenisey R.

SLOVAKIA
HUNGARY
MOLDOVA
ROMANIA
BULGARIA

KIEV

UKRAINE

Don R.

ballet

ox

BLACK SEA

caviar

nomad yurt

TURKEY

CASPIAN SEA

KAZAKHSTAN

ASTANA

TBILISI

GEORGIA

camel

snow leopard

YEREVAN

ARMENIA

BAKU

AZERBAIJAN

Turkmen horseman

TASHKENT

UZBEKISTAN

CHINA

ASHGABAT

BISHKEK

IRAN

cotton

TURKMENISTAN

KYRGYZSTAN

DUSHANBE

AFGHANISTAN

TAJIKISTAN

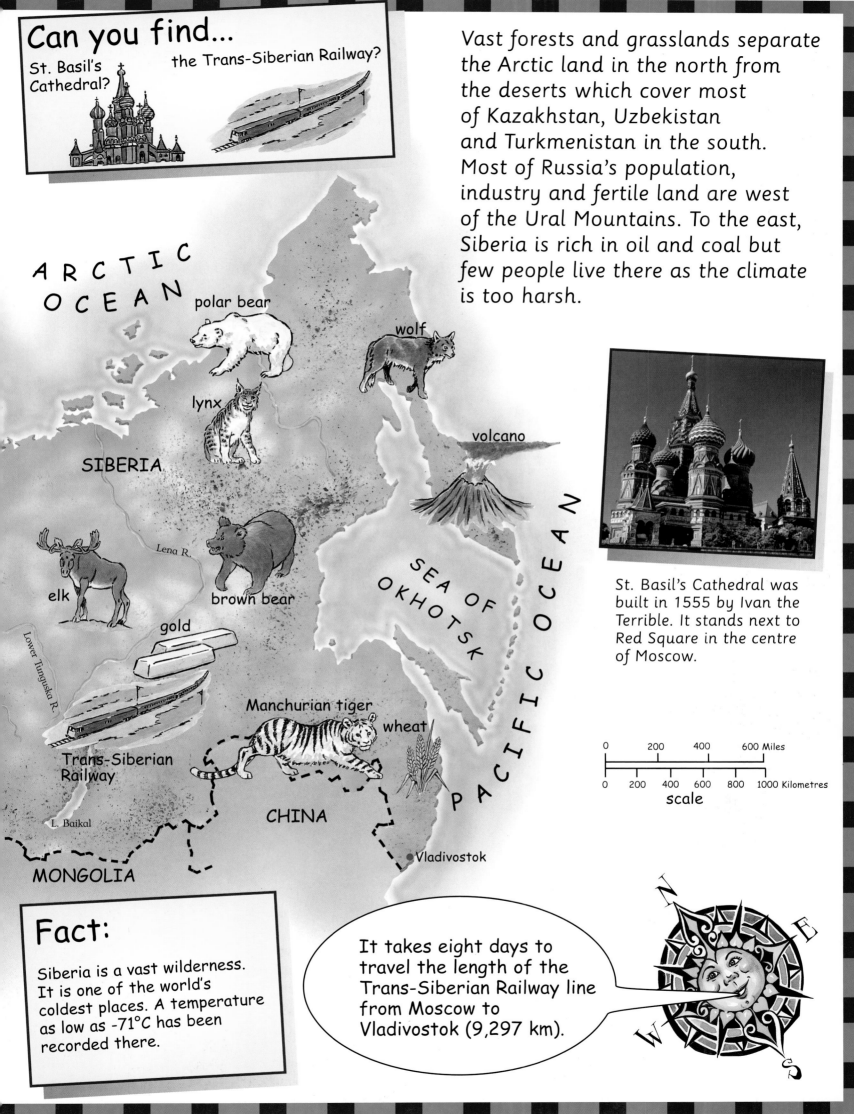

Can you find...

St. Basil's Cathedral?

the Trans-Siberian Railway?

Vast forests and grasslands separate the Arctic land in the north from the deserts which cover most of Kazakhstan, Uzbekistan and Turkmenistan in the south. Most of Russia's population, industry and fertile land are west of the Ural Mountains. To the east, Siberia is rich in oil and coal but few people live there as the climate is too harsh.

ARCTIC OCEAN

polar bear

wolf

lynx

volcano

SIBERIA

Lena R.

brown bear

elk

Lower Tunguska R.

gold

SEA OF OKHOTSK

PACIFIC OCEAN

St. Basil's Cathedral was built in 1555 by Ivan the Terrible. It stands next to Red Square in the centre of Moscow.

Trans-Siberian Railway

Manchurian tiger

wheat

CHINA

L. Baikal

Vladivostok

MONGOLIA

| 0 | 200 | 400 | 600 Miles |

| 0 | 200 | 400 | 600 | 800 | 1000 Kilometres |

scale

Fact:

Siberia is a vast wilderness. It is one of the world's coldest places. A temperature as low as -71°C has been recorded there.

It takes eight days to travel the length of the Trans-Siberian Railway line from Moscow to Vladivostok (9,297 km).

Can you find...

the Royal Tomb at Petra?

the Suleymaniye Mosque?

SOUTH-WEST ASIA

BULGARIA

BLACK SEA

GREECE

Istanbul

TURKEY

■ ANKARA

Suleymaniye Mosque

whirling dervish

Krak des Chevaliers

TURKISH STATE OF CYPRUS

NICOSIA

BEIRUT

CYPRUS

LEBANON

SYRIA

DAMASCUS

WEST BANK (disputed)

■ AMMAN

JERUSALEM

JORDAN

Dome of the Rock

ISRAEL

Dead Sea

EGYPT

Petra

MEDITERRANEAN SEA

scorpion

RED SEA

Mecca

Jeddah

South-West Asia

This area, also known as the Middle East, is mainly hot and dry with vast arid deserts to the south. It is a huge oil-producing region, supplying much of the world's oil.

The Middle East has long been troubled by wars between neighbouring countries. The discovery of large amounts of oil and natural gas around the Persian Gulf has brought great wealth to the region.

Fact:

The Dead Sea lies on the border of Israel and Jordan. Its water is so salty that people can float in it without swimming — it is impossible to sink.

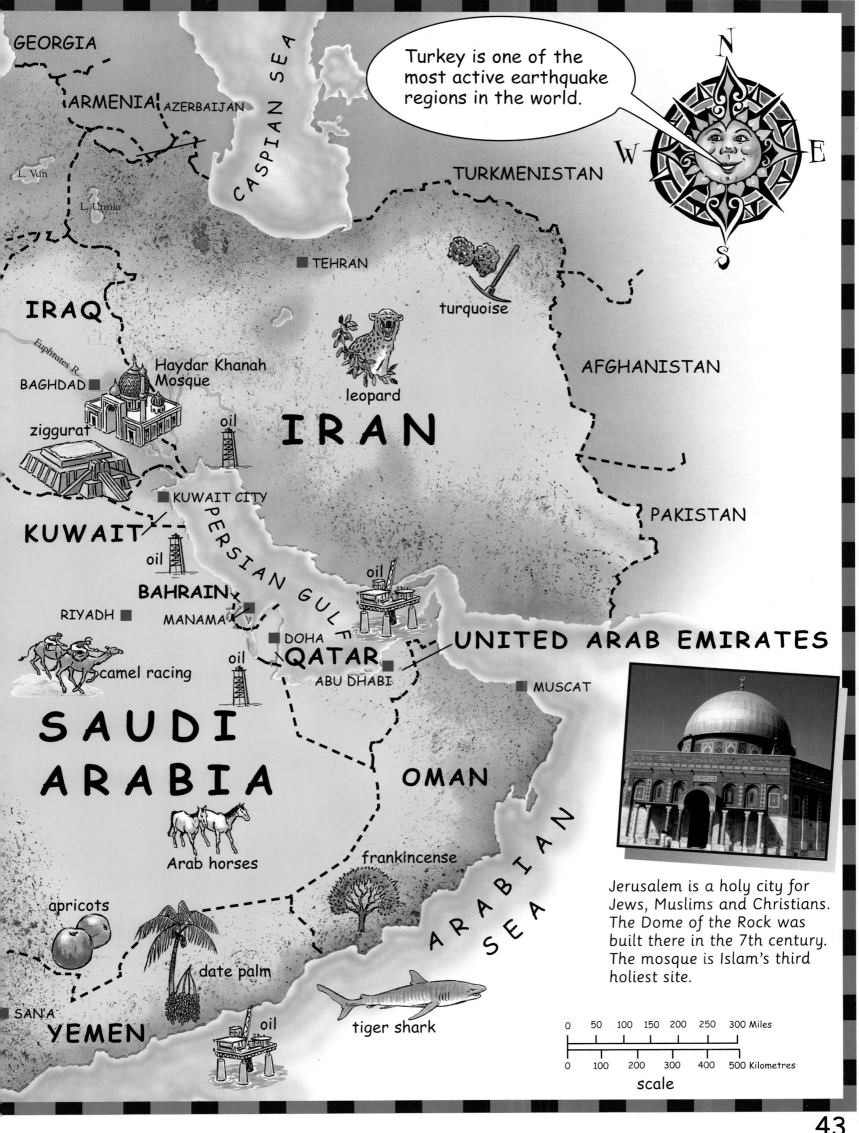

GEORGIA

ARMENIA AZERBAIJAN

CASPIAN SEA

L. Van

L. Urmia

Turkey is one of the most active earthquake regions in the world.

N
W   E
S

TURKMENISTAN

TEHRAN

turquoise

AFGHANISTAN

IRAQ

Euphrates R.

BAGHDAD Haydar Khanah Mosque

ziggurat

leopard

IRAN

oil

PAKISTAN

KUWAIT CITY

KUWAIT

oil

BAHRAIN

RIYADH MANAMA

PERSIAN GULF

oil

DOHA

QATAR

ABU DHABI

UNITED ARAB EMIRATES

MUSCAT

camel racing

SAUDI ARABIA

oil

OMAN

Arab horses

apricots

frankincense

ARABIAN SEA

Jerusalem is a holy city for Jews, Muslims and Christians. The Dome of the Rock was built there in the 7th century. The mosque is Islam's third holiest site.

date palm

SAN'A

YEMEN

oil

tiger shark

| 0 | 50 | 100 | 150 | 200 | 250 | 300 Miles |

| 0 | 100 | 200 | 300 | 400 | 500 Kilometres |

scale

NORTHERN AFRICA

Tangier
ALGIERS
TUNIS
RABAT
TUNISIA
CANARY ISLANDS (SPAIN)
MOROCCO
ALGERIA
TRIPOLI
Nomads
LIBYA
WESTERN SAHARA
(disputed)
oil
S A H A R A
dolphins
MAURITANIA
hippopotamus
ostrich
MALI
Niger R.
SENEGAL
NIGER
GAMBIA
DAKAR
BAMAKO
NIAMEY
L. Chad
BANJUL
NOUAKCHOTT
BURKINA FASO
N'DJAMENA
GUINEA-BISSAU
BISSAU
GUINEA
OUAGADOUGOU
NIGERIA
CONAKRY
diamonds
Niger R.
ABUJA
FREETOWN
bananas
A T L A N T I C   O C E A N
SIERRA LEONE
MONROVIA
LIBERIA
GHANA
LOMÉ
PORTO-NOVO
oil
YAOUNDÉ
YAMOUSSOUKRO
ACCRA
IVORY COAST
TOGO
CAMEROON
BENIN
GABON

Northern Africa

Much of the huge continent of Africa is hot and dry. The land along the Mediterranean coast and the Nile Valley is rich and fertile. The vast Sahara Desert covers more than half of north Africa.

Fact:

The Sahara Desert is the largest desert in the world, covering about nine million square kilometres.

Many Africans live in small villages and farm the land. The Nile Valley in Egypt is the most densely populated region. Cairo is Africa's largest city.

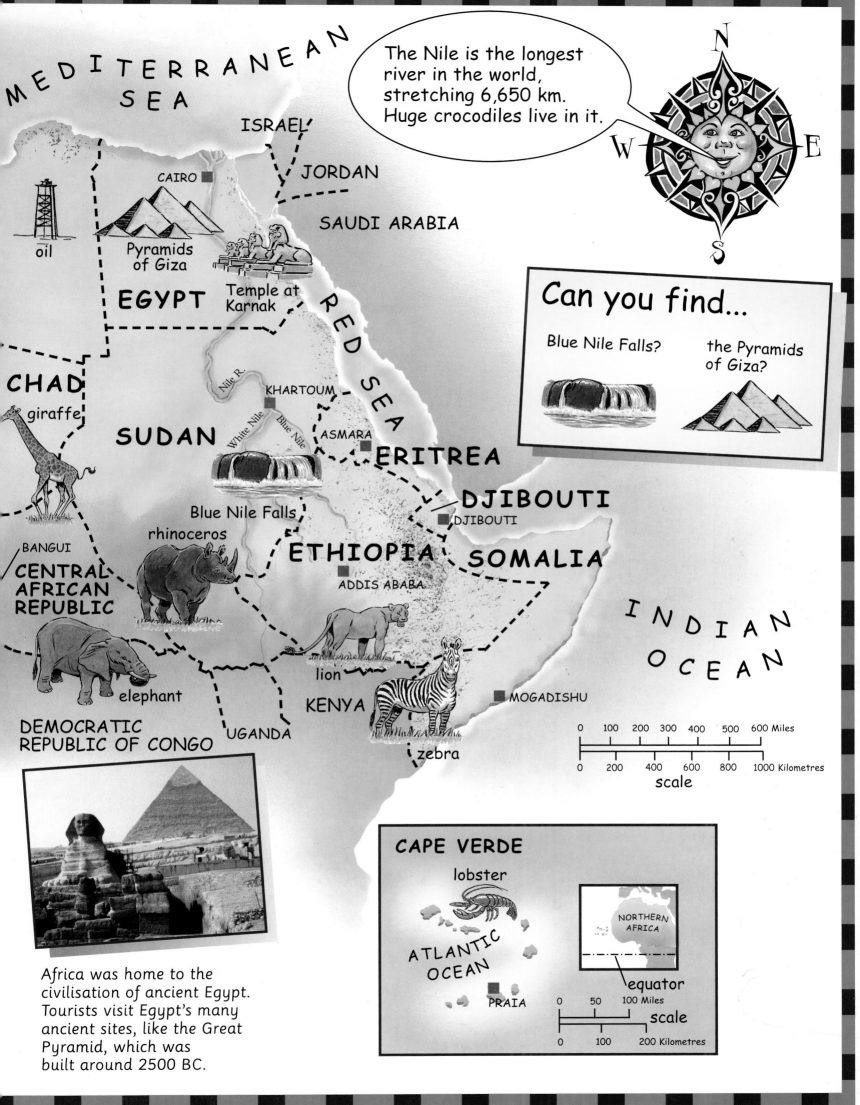

MEDITERRANEAN SEA

ISRAEL

The Nile is the longest river in the world, stretching 6,650 km. Huge crocodiles live in it.

N
W E
S

CAIRO

oil

Pyramids of Giza

EGYPT

Temple at Karnak

JORDAN

SAUDI ARABIA

RED SEA

Can you find...

Blue Nile Falls?   the Pyramids of Giza?

CHAD

giraffe

Nile R.

KHARTOUM

SUDAN

White Nile   Blue Nile

ASMARA

ERITREA

DJIBOUTI

DJIBOUTI

Blue Nile Falls

rhinoceros

BANGUI

CENTRAL AFRICAN REPUBLIC

ETHIOPIA

SOMALIA

ADDIS ABABA

INDIAN OCEAN

elephant

lion

KENYA

zebra

MOGADISHU

DEMOCRATIC REPUBLIC OF CONGO

UGANDA

0   100 200 300 400 500 600 Miles

0   200   400   600   800 1000 Kilometres

scale

Africa was home to the civilisation of ancient Egypt. Tourists visit Egypt's many ancient sites, like the Great Pyramid, which was built around 2500 BC.

CAPE VERDE

lobster

ATLANTIC OCEAN

PRAIA

NORTHERN AFRICA

equator

0   50   100 Miles

0   100   200 Kilometres

scale

The top of Mount Kilimanjaro in Tanzania is covered in snow all year round.

Southern Africa

The mighty Congo River runs through dense, tropical rainforests in Central Africa. Crocodiles, chimpanzees and gorillas live in these hot, steamy forests. Grasslands and deserts make up much of Southern Africa, but there is rich farmland in the far south.

EQUATORIAL GUINEA
MALABO
pygmies
CAMEROON
chimpanzee
LIBREVILLE
GABON
flying fish
CONGO REPUBLIC
BRAZZAVILLE
rainforest
KINSHASA
CABINDA (ANGOLA)
LUANDA
ANGOLA
ATLANTIC OCEAN
diamonds
oil
springbok
meerkats
NAMIBIA
WINDHOEK
diamonds
SOUTH AFRICA
wine
CAPE TOWN

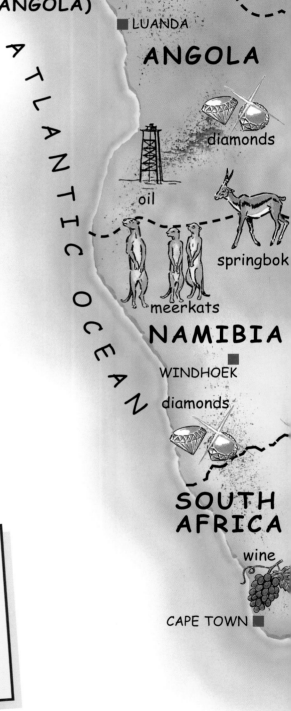

Can you find...

Victoria Falls?

meerkats?

Fact:

Pygmy tribes live deep in the rainforests of Congo. They are a race of people who are usually under 1.5 metres tall.

| 0 | 100 | 200 | 300 | 400 | 500 | 600 Miles |

| 0 | 200 | 400 | 600 | 800 | 1000 Kilometres |

scale

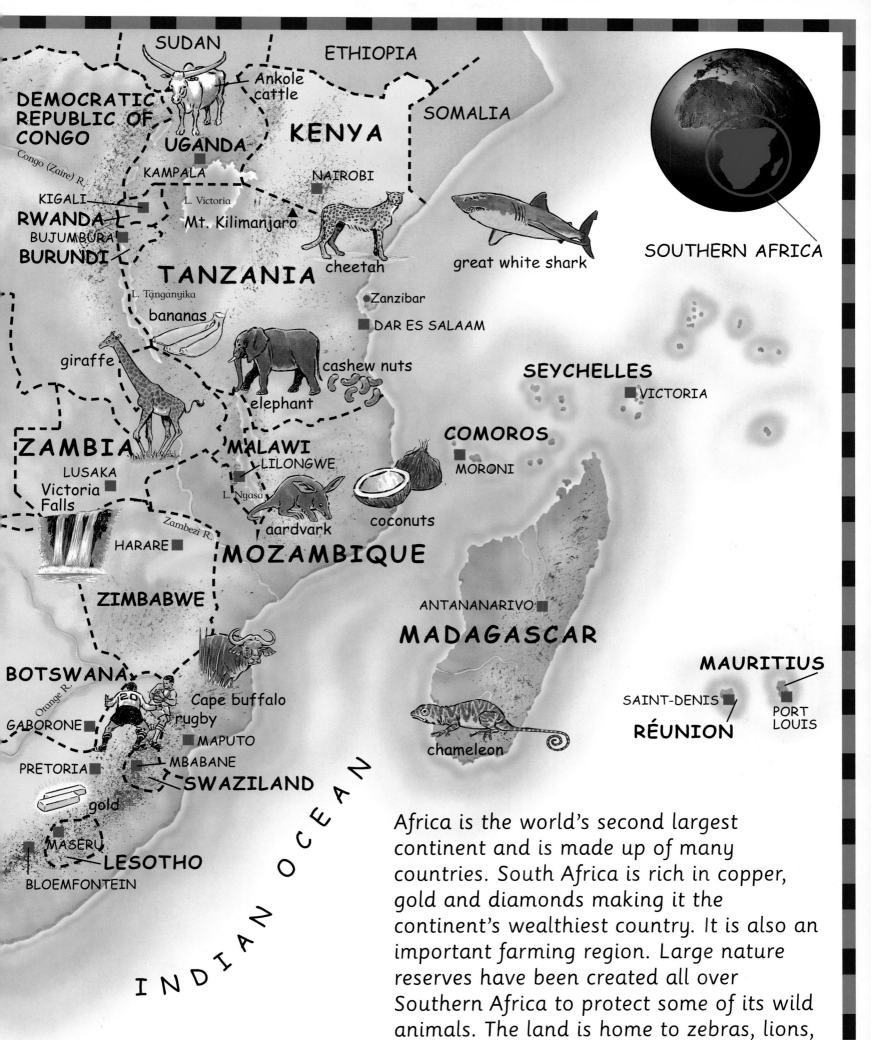

SUDAN
ETHIOPIA
Ankole cattle
DEMOCRATIC REPUBLIC OF CONGO
SOMALIA
SOUTHERN AFRICA
UGANDA
KENYA
Congo (Zaire) R.
KAMPALA
NAIROBI
KIGALI
L. Victoria
RWANDA
Mt. Kilimanjaro
cheetah
great white shark
BUJUMBURA
BURUNDI
TANZANIA
Zanzibar
L. Tanganyika
DAR ES SALAAM
bananas
SEYCHELLES
VICTORIA
giraffe
elephant
cashew nuts
COMOROS
ZAMBIA
MALAWI
MORONI
LUSAKA
LILONGWE
Victoria Falls
L. Nyasa
coconuts
aardvark
HARARE
Zambezi R.
MOZAMBIQUE
ANTANANARIVO
ZIMBABWE
MADAGASCAR
MAURITIUS
BOTSWANA
Cape buffalo
rugby
SAINT-DENIS
PORT LOUIS
GABORONE
MAPUTO
chameleon
RÉUNION
PRETORIA
MBABANE
gold
SWAZILAND
MASERU
LESOTHO
BLOEMFONTEIN
INDIAN OCEAN

Africa is the world's second largest continent and is made up of many countries. South Africa is rich in copper, gold and diamonds making it the continent's wealthiest country. It is also an important farming region. Large nature reserves have been created all over Southern Africa to protect some of its wild animals. The land is home to zebras, lions, cheetahs, leopards, elephants, rhinoceroses, ostriches and giraffes.

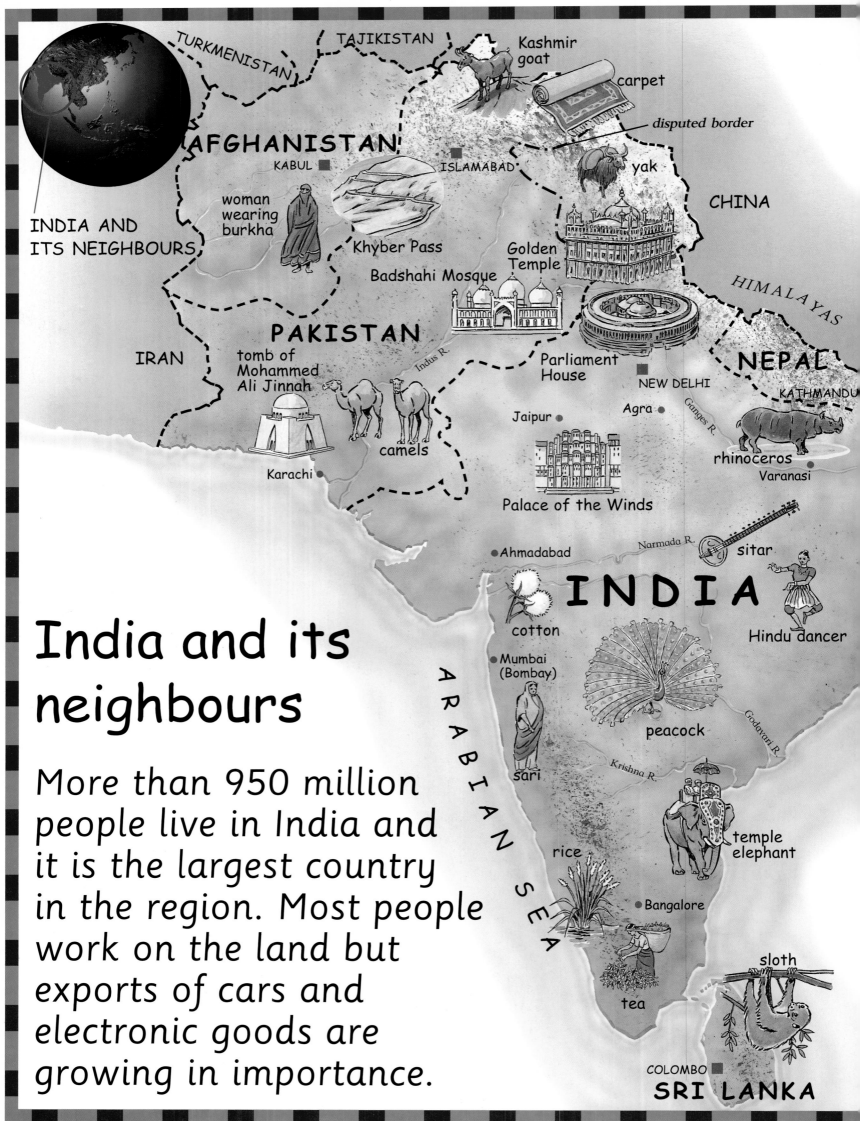

TURKMENISTAN
TAJIKISTAN
Kashmir goat
carpet
disputed border

INDIA AND
ITS NEIGHBOURS

AFGHANISTAN
KABUL
ISLAMABAD
yak
CHINA

woman
wearing
burkha
Khyber Pass
Golden
Temple
HIMALAYAS

Badshahi Mosque

PAKISTAN

IRAN
tomb of
Mohammed
Ali Jinnah
Indus R.
Parliament
House
NEW DELHI
NEPAL
KATHMANDU

camels
Jaipur
Agra
Ganges R.

Karachi
Palace of the Winds
rhinoceros
Varanasi

Ahmadabad
Narmada R.
sitar

cotton
INDIA
Hindu dancer

Mumbai
(Bombay)
peacock
Godavari R.

India and its neighbours

A
R
A
B
I
A
N

S
E
A
sari
Krishna R.

More than 950 million
people live in India and
it is the largest country
in the region. Most people
work on the land but
exports of cars and
electronic goods are
growing in importance.

rice
temple
elephant

Bangalore

sloth

tea

COLOMBO
SRI LANKA

48

Can you find...

the Palace of the Winds?

the Golden Temple?

a temple elephant?

Vast mountain ranges separate this region from Central Asia. The climate is hot and dry, so many people live on the coast or on the fertile plains along the Ganges and Indus rivers. India, Bangladesh and Sri Lanka are some of the world's main tea-growing nations. Most industries are concentrated in India and Pakistan's large, crowded cities.

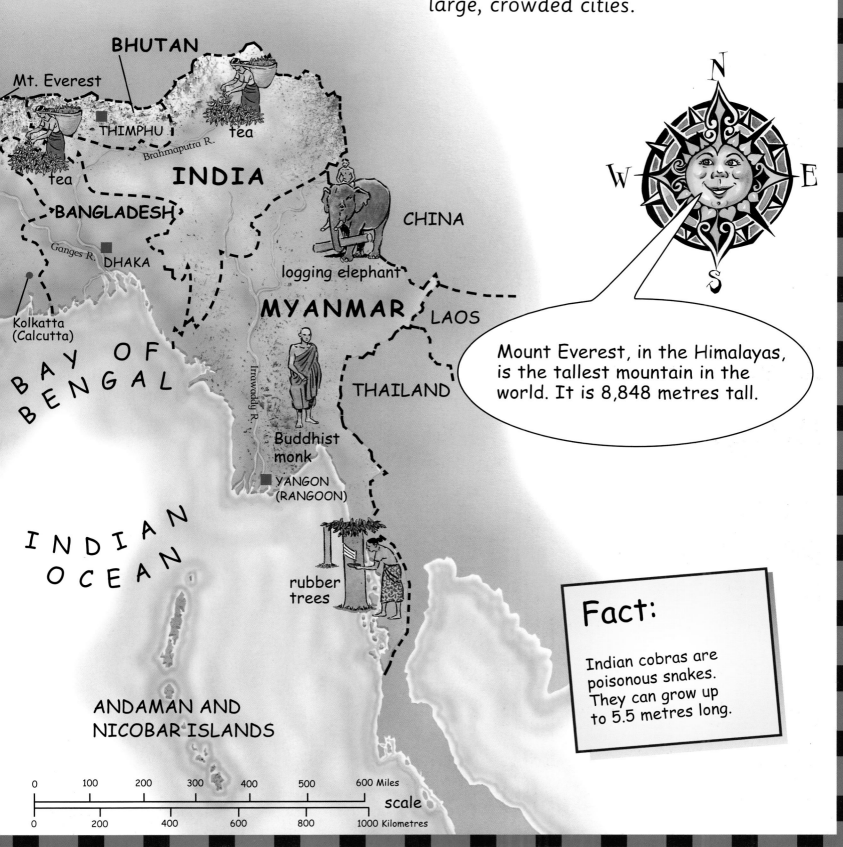

BHUTAN

Mt. Everest

THIMPHU

tea

Brahmaputra R.

INDIA

tea

BANGLADESH

Ganges R.

DHAKA

Kolkatta (Calcutta)

BAY OF BENGAL

CHINA

logging elephant

MYANMAR

LAOS

Irrawaddy R.

THAILAND

Buddhist monk

YANGON (RANGOON)

INDIAN OCEAN

rubber trees

N

W   E

S

Mount Everest, in the Himalayas, is the tallest mountain in the world. It is 8,848 metres tall.

Fact:

Indian cobras are poisonous snakes. They can grow up to 5.5 metres long.

ANDAMAN AND NICOBAR ISLANDS

| 0 | 100 | 200 | 300 | 400 | 500 | 600 Miles |

scale

| 0 | 200 | 400 | 600 | 800 | 1000 Kilometres |

49

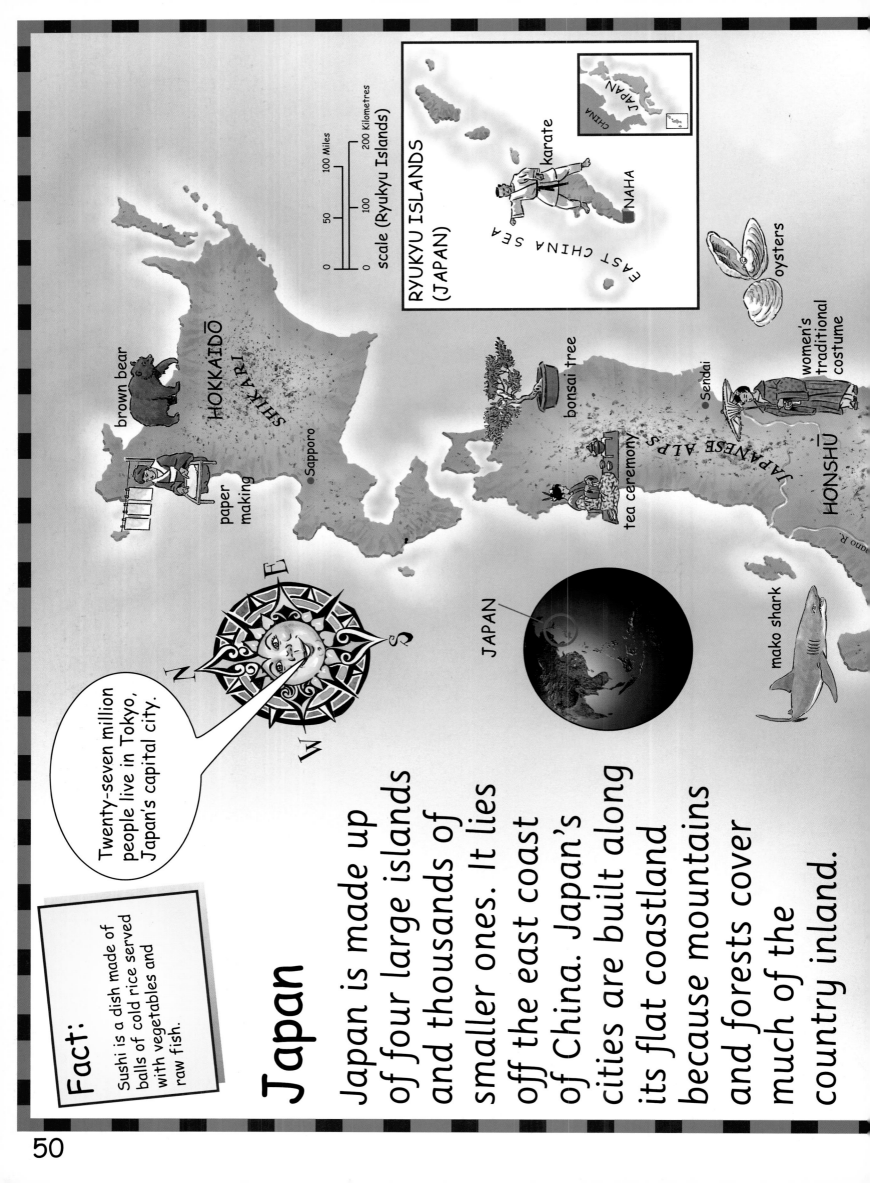

Japan

Japan is made up of four large islands and thousands of smaller ones. It lies off the east coast of China. Japan's cities are built along its flat coastland because mountains and forests cover much of the country inland.

Fact:
Sushi is a dish made of cold rice served balls of with vegetables and raw fish.

Twenty-seven million people live in Tokyo, Japan's capital city.

RYUKYU ISLANDS (JAPAN)

EAST CHINA SEA

karate

NAHA

CHINA

JAPAN

scale (Ryukyu Islands)

200 Kilometres

100 Miles

0

50

100

oysters

brown bear

HOKKAIDŌ

SHIKARI

Sapporo

paper making

bonsai tree

tea ceremony

JAPANESE ALPS

Sendai

women's traditional costume

HONSHŪ

JAPAN

mako shark

N E S W

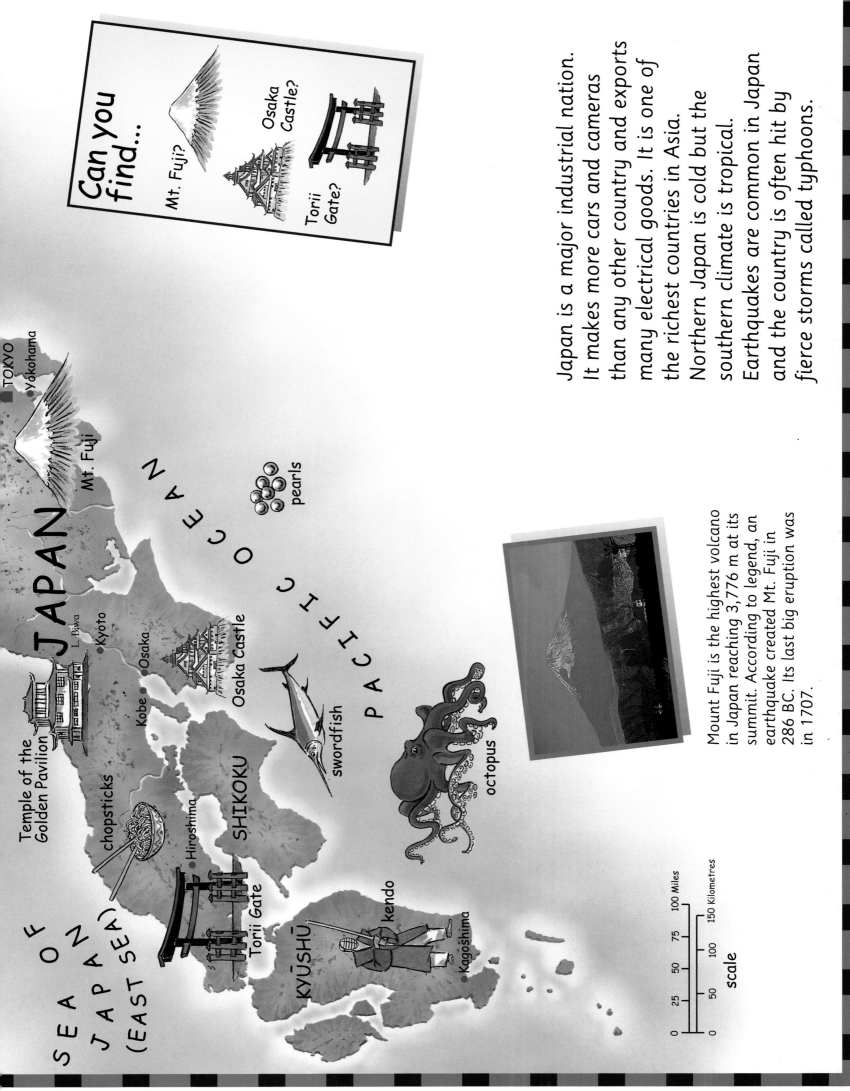

Japan is a major industrial nation. It makes more cars and cameras than any other country and exports many electrical goods. It is one of the richest countries in Asia. Northern Japan is cold but the southern climate is tropical. Earthquakes are common in Japan and the country is often hit by fierce storms called typhoons.

Can you find...

Mt. Fuji?

Osaka Castle?

Torii Gate?

Mount Fuji is the highest volcano in Japan reaching 3,776 m at its summit. According to legend, an earthquake created Mt. Fuji in 286 BC. Its last big eruption was in 1707.

TOKYO
Yokohama

Mt. Fuji

JAPAN

SEA OF JAPAN (EAST SEA)

PACIFIC OCEAN

pearls

L. Biwa
Kyoto

Temple of the Golden Pavilion

chopsticks

Kobe
Osaka

Osaka Castle

swordfish

Hiroshima

SHIKOKU

octopus

Torii Gate

KYŪSHŪ

kendo

Kagoshima

scale

| 0 | 25 | 50 | 75 | 100 Miles |
| 0 | 50 | 100 | 150 Kilometres |

Oil-rich Brunei is one of the world's smallest and wealthiest countries.

Southeast Asia

Southeast Asia is made up of two small areas of mainland and almost 20,000 islands. The climate is hot and humid. Tropical rainforests cover much of this mountainous region and provide the world with most of its hardwoods.

CHINA

elephant

VIETNAM

HANOI

MYANMAR

LAOS

VIENTIANE

folk dancer

THAILAND

BANGKOK

Angkor Wat

CAMBODIA

PHNOM PENH

Ho Chi Minh City

ANDAMAN SEA

rubber tree

leather back turtle

MALAYSIA

KUALA LUMPUR

SINGAPORE

tiger

SUMATRA

tea

INDIAN OCEAN

JAKARTA

JAVA

Can you find...

Angkor Wat?

the skyscrapers of Singapore?

SOUTHEAST ASIA

tiger shark

swordfish

■ MANILA

PHILIPPINES

pineapple

MINDANAO

In remote areas of Southeast Asia people live in houses raised on stilts to avoid being flooded during the rainy season. Monsoon rains fall from June to October. The climate is ideal for growing rice, Southeast Asia's main crop. Pineapples, bananas, mangoes and coconuts are also grown.
The rainforests are rich in plantlife and are home to orang-utans, rhinoceroses, leopards and tigers.

BRUNEI
BANDAR SERI BEGAWAN

MALAYSIA

head hunter with blowpipe

P A C I F I C   O C E A N

| 0 | 100 | 200 | 300 | 400 | 500 | 600 Miles |
| 0 | 200 | 400 | 600 | 800 | 1000 Kilometres |

scale

BORNEO

rice

CELEBES

coconuts

coffee

oil rig

house on stilts

IRIAN JAYA

PAPUA NEW GUINEA

I N D O N E S I A

Borobudur Temple

shadow puppet

Komodo dragon

TIMOR

hammerhead shark

AUSTRALIA

China, Mongolia, Korea and Taiwan

CHINA, MONGOLIA, KOREA AND TAIWAN

More people live in China than in any other country on Earth. Most of the population farm the fertile land in the east, growing rice, wheat, maize and tea. China is also an industrial nation and has many large cities.

High mountain ranges separate China from India and there are vast deserts to the north. The Korean peninsula is divided into North and South Korea. South Korea and the island of Taiwan have successful industries including textiles, cars and electrical goods.

KAZAKHSTAN

oil

wheat

KYRGYZSTAN

cotton

TAJIKISTAN

jade

PAKISTAN

giant panda

INDIA

XIZANG (TIBET)

Tibetan monk

HIMALAYAS

NEPAL

BHUT

INDIA

The Great Wall of China is 3,460 km long. It is the only man-made structure that can be seen from the Moon.

Can you find...

the Forbidden City?

the Potala Palace?

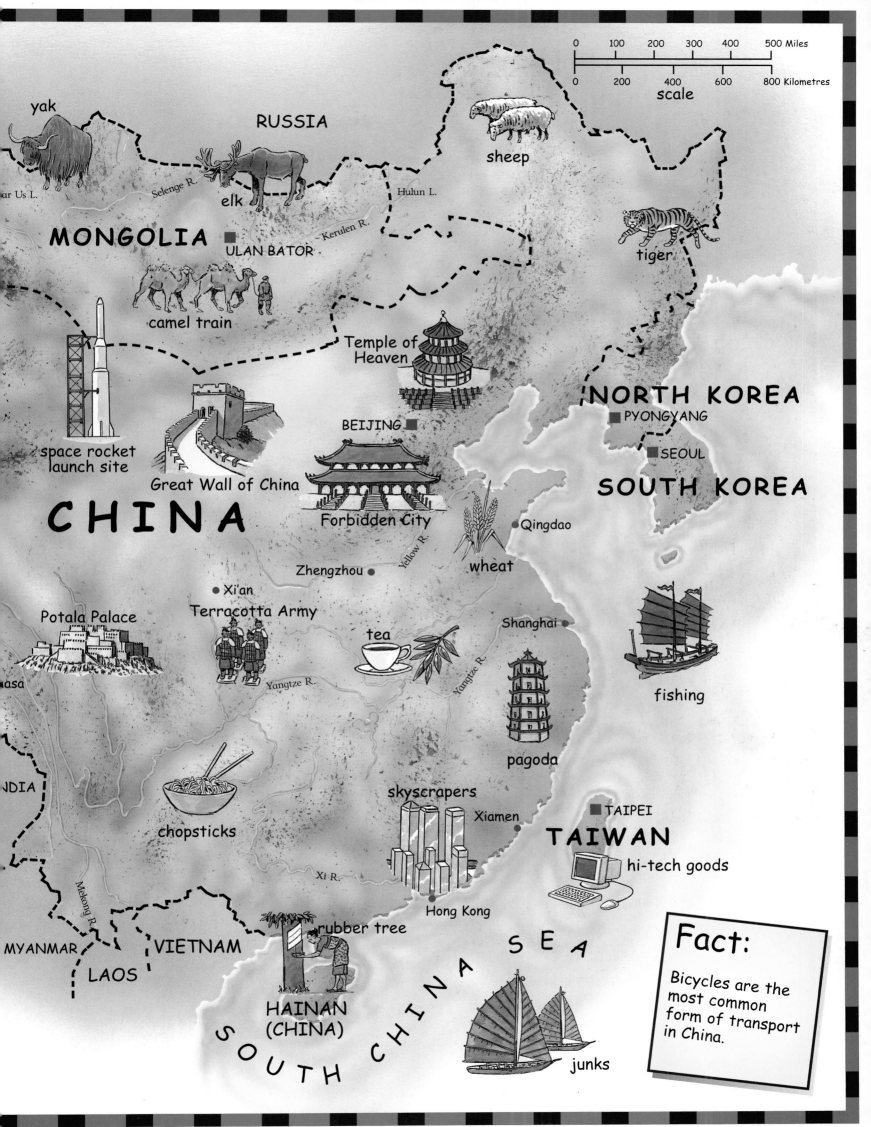

yak

RUSSIA

sheep

elk

Hulun L.

tiger

MONGOLIA

ar Us L.

Selenge R.

Kerulen R.

ULAN BATOR

camel train

space rocket
launch site

Great Wall of China

Temple of
Heaven

BEIJING

Forbidden City

NORTH KOREA

PYONGYANG

SEOUL

SOUTH KOREA

CHINA

Qingdao

wheat

Yellow R.

Zhengzhou

Potala Palace

Xi'an

Terracotta Army

tea

Shanghai

asa

Yangtze R.

Yangtze R.

fishing

pagoda

NDIA

chopsticks

skyscrapers

Xiamen

TAIPEI

TAIWAN

hi-tech goods

Xi R.

Hong Kong

rubber tree

MYANMAR

VIETNAM

LAOS

HAINAN
(CHINA)

S O U T H   C H I N A   S E A

junks

Mekong R.

scale

0   100   200   300   400   500 Miles

0   200   400   600   800 Kilometres

Fact:

Bicycles are the
most common
form of transport
in China.

AUSTRALIA AND
PAPUA NEW GUINEA

Papua New Guinea has
over 700 languages – more
than any other country.

traditional dancer

gold

PORT MORESBY

PAPUA NEW GUINEA

| 0 | 100 | 200 | 300 | 400 | 500 | 600 Miles |

| 0 | 200 | 400 | 600 | 800 | 1000 Kilometres |

scale (Papua New Guinea)

AUSTRALIA

Australia and Papua New Guinea

Australia is the world's smallest continent. It is a large, wealthy country with a small population. It is hot and dry inland so most people live in large coastal cities. Much of Australia's wealth comes from farming, mining and tourism.

Central Australia is called the 'outback'. It is mainly deserts and grasslands. Few people live there, but vast numbers of sheep and cattle graze on stations (farms). Australia produces more wool than any other country. It also has large deposits of opals, diamonds, gold and silver.

| 0 | 100 | 200 | 300 | 400 | 500 | 600 Miles |

| 0 | 200 | 400 | 600 | 800 | 1000 Kilometres |

scale

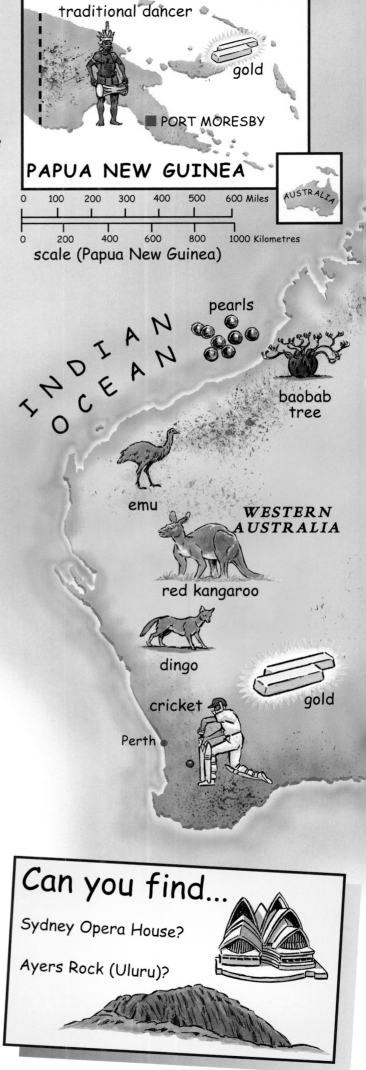

INDIAN OCEAN

pearls

baobab tree

emu

WESTERN AUSTRALIA

red kangaroo

dingo

cricket

gold

Perth

Can you find...

Sydney Opera House?

Ayers Rock (Uluru)?

The Great Barrier Reef is made of coral. It is so big that it can be seen from the Moon.

N
W E
S

GREAT BARRIER REEF

PACIFIC OCEAN

Darwin

Aboriginal dancers

diamonds

salt-water crocodile

meteorite crater

cattle

green turtle

NORTHERN TERRITORY

wallabies

flying doctors

pineapple

QUEENSLAND

termite mound

Ayers Rock (Uluru)

AUSTRALIA

skyscrapers

Brisbane

SOUTH AUSTRALIA

opals

koala

surfing

Indian-Pacific Railway

wine

sheep

Darling R.

NEW SOUTH WALES

Murrumbidgee R.

Sydney Opera House

great white shark

Murray R.

Murray R.

Adelaide

Sydney

CANBERRA (capital)

grey kangaroos

VICTORIA

Melbourne

Tasmanian devil

Fact:

In Australia, people who live a long way from hospitals depend on the Flying Doctor service when they need medical help. The service allows doctors to travel great distances quickly by aeroplane.

TASMANIA

Hobart

New Zealand

New Zealand is divided into two islands. Most people live on its volcanic North Island. It has large cattle and sheep ranches and exports dairy produce and lamb.

0   50   100   150   200   250 Miles

0   100   200   300   400 Kilometres

scale

kauri tree

kiwi fruit

Auckland

Hamilton

oil rig

Maori war dance

L. Taupo

NORTH ISLAND

Parliament House

barracuda

N E W
Z E A L A N D

WELLINGTON

N
W   E
S

Maoris were the first people to settle in New Zealand.

NEW ZEALAND

T A S M A N   S E A

sheep

SOUTH ISLAND

sheep

rugby

Dunedin

oysters

Christchurch Cathedral

Rakaia R.

Christchurch

P A C I F I C   O C E A N

blue whale

Fact:
There are more sheep than people in New Zealand.

Can you find...

Parliament House?

Christchurch Cathedral?

58

South Western Pacific Islands

Thousands of small tropical islands are scattered across the Pacific Ocean, east of Australia. Most islanders live in small villages. They fish and grow tropical fruit, including bananas and coconuts.

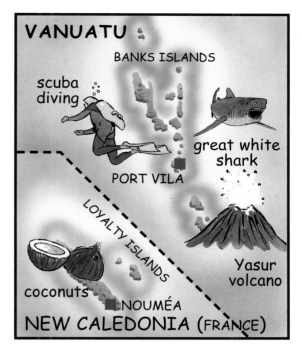

VANUATU
BANKS ISLANDS
scuba diving
great white shark
PORT VILA
LOYALTY ISLANDS
coconuts
Yasur volcano
NOUMÉA
NEW CALEDONIA (FRANCE)

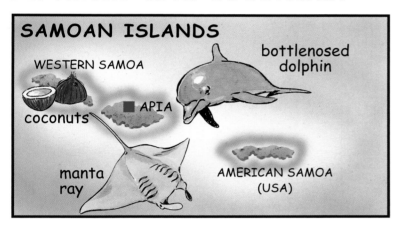

SAMOAN ISLANDS
WESTERN SAMOA
bottlenosed dolphin
coconuts
APIA
manta ray
AMERICAN SAMOA (USA)

BOUGAINVILLE
house on stilts
NEW GEORGIA ISLANDS
HONIARA
bananas
SANTA CRUZ ISLANDS
SOLOMON ISLANDS

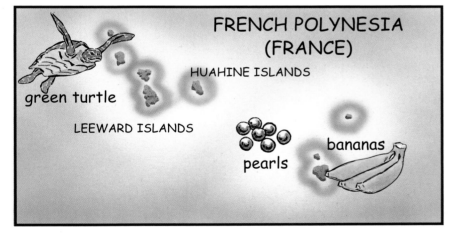

FRENCH POLYNESIA (FRANCE)
HUAHINE ISLANDS
green turtle
LEEWARD ISLANDS
pearls
bananas

Fact:

The people of Bougainville in the Solomon Islands have discovered how to use coconut oil as a fuel for motor cars.

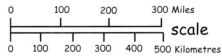

0   100   200   300 Miles
scale
0 100 200 300 400 500 Kilometres

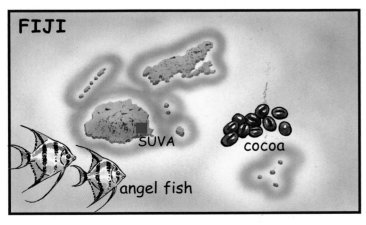

FIJI
SUVA
cocoa
angel fish

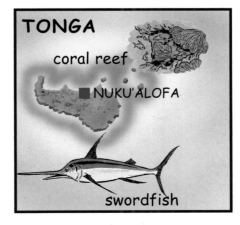

TONGA
coral reef
NUKU'ALOFA
swordfish

SOUTH WESTERN PACIFIC ISLANDS

The Arctic

The Arctic Ocean is covered in thick ice at the North Pole. The Inuit and Sami are the only people who live in this harsh environment, but many animals and plants survive there.

THE ARCTIC

Fact:
Polar bears can grow up to 3 m tall. They are the largest type of bear in the world.

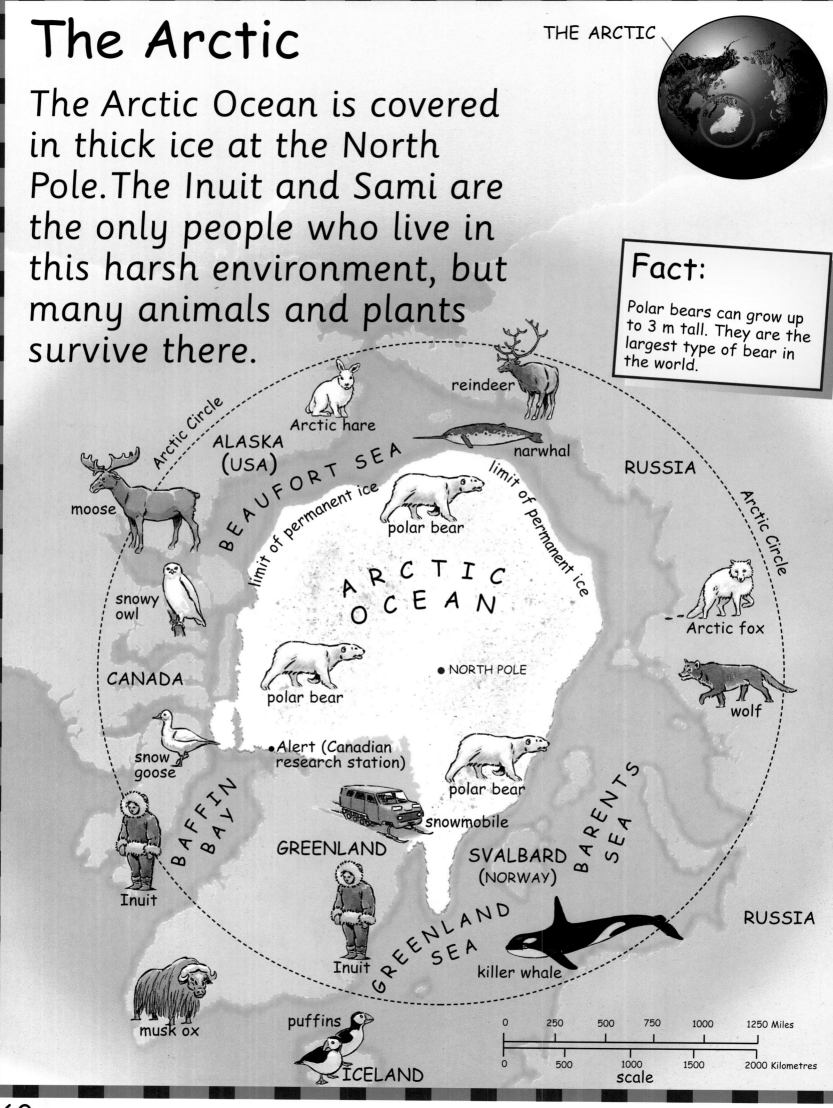

Arctic Circle

Arctic hare

ALASKA (USA)

reindeer

BEAUFORT SEA

narwhal

RUSSIA

limit of permanent ice

limit of permanent ice

Arctic Circle

moose

polar bear

ARCTIC OCEAN

snowy owl

Arctic fox

CANADA

polar bear

NORTH POLE

wolf

snow goose

Alert (Canadian research station)

polar bear

BAFFIN BAY

snowmobile

BARENTS SEA

Inuit

GREENLAND

SVALBARD (NORWAY)

GREENLAND SEA

RUSSIA

Inuit

killer whale

musk ox

puffins

ICELAND

| 0 | 250 | 500 | 750 | 1000 | 1250 Miles |

| 0 | 500 | 1000 | 1500 | 2000 Kilometres |

scale

The Antarctic

The South Pole in the Antarctic is the coldest place on Earth. No country owns this frozen continent but many have set up scientific research stations there.

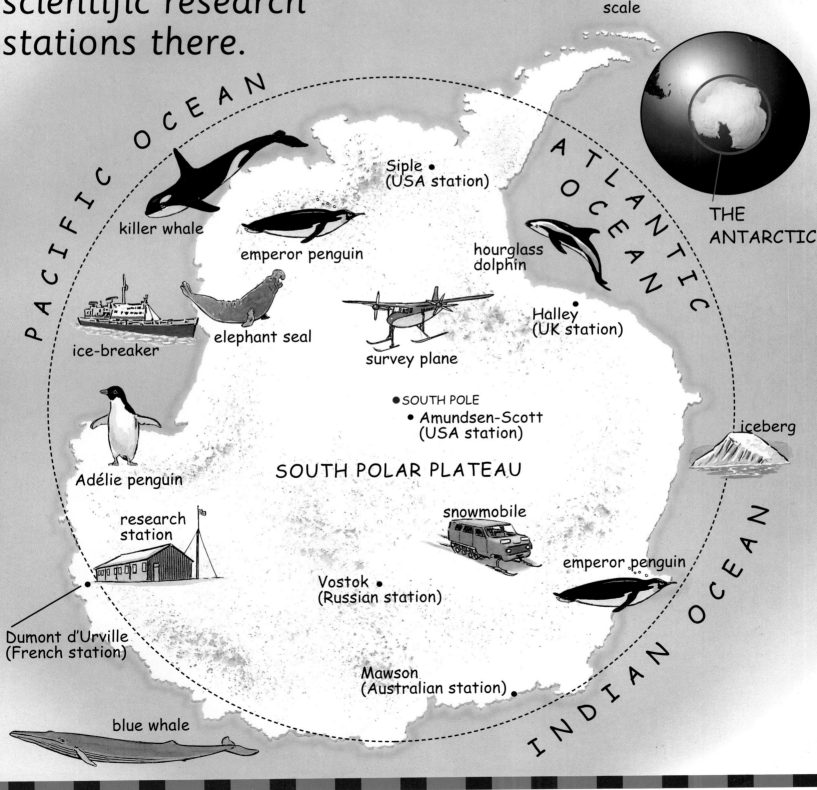

scale

0   250   500   750   1000   1250 Miles

0   500   1000   1500   2000 Kilometres

THE ANTARCTIC

PACIFIC OCEAN

ATLANTIC OCEAN

INDIAN OCEAN

killer whale

Siple •
(USA station)

emperor penguin

hourglass dolphin

ice-breaker

elephant seal

survey plane

Halley •
(UK station)

iceberg

Adélie penguin

•SOUTH POLE
• Amundsen-Scott
(USA station)

SOUTH POLAR PLATEAU

research station

snowmobile

emperor penguin

Vostok •
(Russian station)

Dumont d'Urville
(French station)

Mawson
(Australian station) •

blue whale

Glossary

climate The average weather of a region.

continent One of the large masses of land on the Earth's surface.

desert An area that has very little or no rainfall.

equator The imaginary line around the centre of the Earth. The areas around the equator are the parts of the planet closest to the Sun.

export Something that is sent from one country to be sold in another.

fertile Soil that will grow plenty of crops.

humid Warm and damp.

hurricane A storm with very strong winds.

independence A country ruled by another country gains independence when it begins ruling itself.

latitude Imaginary lines that run horizontally around the Earth.

longitude Imaginary lines that run vertically around the Earth.

map projection The process of forming a flat atlas map by 'stretching' a globe.

monsoon A strong South-Asian wind that usually also brings heavy rain.

northern hemisphere The half of the Earth north of the equator.

peninsula A narrow area of land that sticks out far into the sea.

permanent Something that will last.

population The people who live in a place or country.

southern hemisphere The half of the Earth south of the equator.

summit The highest point of a mountain.

tropical Very warm and humid conditions, as found in the areas around the equator.

volcanic Anything formed by a volcano.

Index

Editors: Karen Barker Smith
                      Stephanie Cole

Picture Research: Nicola Roe

Consultant: Penny Clarke

Photographic credits
Digital Stock/Corbis Corporation: 20, 25, 32, 35, 37, 41
John Foxx Images: 29, 31, 43, 45
Pictor International: 10, 17, 26, 51
Salariya Book Company: 15

Printed on paper from sustainable forests.

Printed and bound in China.

ISBN 978 0 7502 4277 6

Created, designed and produced by
The Salariya Book Company Ltd
Book House, 25 Marlborough Place,
Brighton BN1 1UB

Visit the Salariya Book Company at **www.salariya.com**

Published in Great Britain in 2002 by Hodder Wayland,
an imprint of Hodder Children's Books
First published in paperback in 2005
Reprinted in 2007 by Wayland, an imprint of Hachette Children's Books
A catalogue record for this book is available from the British Library.

Hachette Children's Books 338 Euston Road, London NW1 3BH